NATURAL RIDING

Natural Riding

Audrey Townley

The Crowood Press

First published in 1990 by
The Crowood Press Ltd
Ramsbury, Marlborough
Wiltshire SN8 2HR

www.crowood.com

Paperback edition 2003

British Library Cataloguing-in-Publication Data
A catalogue record for this book is available from the British Library.

ISBN 1 86126 570 0

Dedication
I wish to dedicate this book to my brother Denis and the Beaver,
also to my dear friends Anna and Jean.

Typeset by Alacrity Phototypesetters, Weston-super-Mare, Avon.
Printed and bound in Great Britain by The Cromwell Press, Trowbridge

Contents

Foreword

Audrey Townley is a gifted teacher in the art of equitation, but even experts can come up against problems that are difficult to solve.

Audrey felt there were instances where the full potential of rider and horse were denied through a lack of understanding between rider and mount, causing frustration to the dedicated learner who would unwittingly stand in the way of his or her own advancement. This problem caused Audrey to search for ways and means of devising a teaching method which would produce patience and serenity of mind so that these qualities, combined with knowledge, would produce the sensitivity which is the foundation of the good equestrian.

The result of Audrey's search was Tim Gallwey's 'Inner Game' coaching. This is a new concept of learning: an adaptive process which concentrates the mind on relationships – in this case not with an inanimate subject but between rider and living horse. The rider becomes thoughtful – 'full wise is he that can himselven know'. He or she searches within himself or herself for answers to problems, listens to what the horse has to say and realises that the horse is a good communicator if it is simply allowed to be – with its highly developed senses it was always the better listener. If this method is followed, a rapport must surely be the outcome.

I have read the manuscript for this book with pleasure. It is full of information but, above all, there is so much common sense in it for the instructor or rider who is prepared to try a new approach, releasing the mind from the trammels of anxieties and tensions and setting it upon observation and intuition. They will realise that there is a language to be learnt by horse and rider to the benefit of both – not only to become more efficient, but to gain that true partnership of the successful rider and the happy horse.

Margaret Wyper
President, British Horse Society,
  Grampian Region
President, Pony Clubs Area 1 Branches
Riding Establishments Act
  Representative
Guy Cubitt Award
BHS Award of Merit

Acknowledgements

I am deeply indebted to the team of experts and special friends who have been responsible for making this book into a fact, instead of it remaining a fantasy. I wish to thank in particular my editor John Button for his invaluable help throughout, also Terence Leigh who painstakingly and skilfully produced the photographs. My gratitude also goes to Vivien Chapman who drew the clear and lively illustrations and to Janet Sparrow for the diagrams. Next, I offer my special thanks to Elsie Paterson who spent hours patiently deciphering my writing and transformed the text into a manuscript.

It is my pupils and their horses who have created the theme for the book and have given me the inspiration I needed to write it, so they have my gratitude. I wish to thank The Grove Riding Centre, Aberdeen and The Deep Water School of Equitation, Dumfries for so generously providing the riders and horses for the photographs. In addition, I would like to thank Margaret Wyper for kindly consenting to write the Foreword.

Finally, may I thank those at The Crowood Press for bringing the whole project into print. I should like to think that this book represents our joint tribute to the Horse, who has served us faithfully from time immemorial.

Preface to the Paperback Edition

I feel that it is appropriate in this new edition to say a little about how the natural riding approach has recently benefited riders and their horses.

After I had retired my great-nephew Curtis came to stay, and during his visit he asked me if I could help him with his riding. Although very keen, he was still having problems. His mother, a physiotherapist, checked his back to see if the pain he suffered after riding was one of the causes of his problems.

I was able to hire a local school and one of their horses. The facilities were strange to Curtis, and my approach to teaching would also be new to him. My priority was therefore to reduce the tension this situation would cause. I explained that my aim for him was comfort and enjoyment. I would avoid all judgement, and ask him to pay attention to just one thing at a time and to listen carefully to what his body and that of the horse were telling him.

The first step was to make friends with the horse in a leisurely way and with his full attention. I call this 'making friends'. The next step was to encourage him to find a comfortable way of sitting in the saddle, and to forget about trying to do it the 'correct way'. Once he had a degree of confidence, I encouraged him to walk round the school and familiarize himself with its proportions, space and appearance. This gave me the chance to observe his body language and that of his horse. What was immediately obvious was a rigidity which is often displayed by a conventionally taught rider. I waited until he turned in to report my observations.

This exercise provided the opportunity for him to notice that certain areas of his body were tense. We discussed which area he would like to work on first, so that I could give him a specific exercise to keep him focused with interest instead of effort. When doing this sort of work it is important to be single-minded and work on just one issue at a time. He quickly caught on, and was soon able to estimate his own improvement by giving his increased awareness marks out of ten.

This proved very successful, and soon he was aware of improvements in parts of his body other than the initial problem area. By letting him do the choosing, he had intuitively chosen the root cause of his general stiffness, and was soon able to move on with more freedom to work his horse with fluency. His final summing up of a successful lesson was that he had learnt to relax. After his next lesson when he was home again, I heard that the instructor had commented on his improvement and asked how he had achieved it. Curtis told her what had happened in his lesson with me, and to the instructor's credit the idea was introduced to the whole class. Curtis went on to achieve a high mark of 80 per cent for the practical riding part of his GCSE exam.

During the three years since I was able to show Curtis the way to self-help, much credit is due to the instructors who have developed his potential. Credit also goes to Curtis for his determination and perseverance. I wish him well as he considers the various options in his life, one of which is the option of training for the mounted police.

I would like to conclude with one anonymous quotation, followed by one of my own:

'Doing one thing at a time eases the way to doing many.'

'Scatterbrain attention blocks potential. Single-minded attention is the key to releasing it.'

Introduction

Natural Riding is based on a coaching technique called 'Inner Game' which has been developed over the last fifteen years by Timothy Gallwey. Tim, an American tennis coach, noticed that the harder his pupils tried, the less well they tended to perform. Many coaches now agree with Tim Gallwey that 85 per cent of learning problems are caused by tension which is often related to our tendency to be negative about ourselves. Tension and negativity interfere not only with our particular sport but with our true potential and the quality of our whole life.

Tim Gallwey evolved a process which alleviated this conflict by focusing the pupil's attention very specifically on one area – the ball, the racket, a part of the body, a section of the court. He did not teach as such; instead he asked pupils to feel what was happening to them. As the busy mind paid attention to one factor at a time, awareness of what was actually going on developed, and the body relaxed and could perform naturally. Such was the success of this method that it has now been applied to skiing, golf, business management and music. The Inner Game technique can be used for any situation where stress impinges on performance, as many top athletes are discovering. It was noticed that as awareness increased, so did enjoyment, confidence and achievement.

The aim of *Natural Riding* is to promote a situation which gives the rider a sense of freedom from dos and don'ts of over-instruction in a judgemental environment with its inhibiting effects. When relaxation and self-confidence are experienced through new awareness, time and space take on different dimensions and possibilities while the horse emerges as a true partner and teacher of the game.

Looking back over my working life as a riding instructor, it becomes clear to me that my teaching methods have undergone several changes. When I was newly qualified at the age of seventeen, in the days when it was unusual for women to take up a career with horses, I was tremendously enthusiastic even though I was still regarded with scepticism by the hunting fraternity.

As a child, my own riding lessons had been more trial and error than anything else. I still have recollections of being dragged along on a leading rein bumping against the instructor's horse.

After the War, the British Horse Society revised the examination system. It was in this post-War era that I had the good fortune to become a pupil of the late Captain Edy Goldman to whom I owe so much.

My teaching methods at that time were distinctly authoritarian. Later, I became interested in education in a more general sense and, with the stimulus of teacher friends and physical education specialists, I made radical changes in my methods. This, I felt, created a much improved learning environment. From then onwards I became increasingly interested in facilitating learning for my pupils rather than in simply telling them what to do.

It seems strange that the biggest change of all should have come so late in my life. I had already been teaching for many years when I came across Tim Gallwey's 'Inner Game' coaching, a technique which he has used successfully for teaching such diverse skills as tennis, golf, skiing, business management and public speaking. I attended an Inner Game tennis coaches' course run by Sir John Whitmore and Alan Fine at Darlington and they very soon convinced me of its value. Since then, I have attended three more courses run by Alan Fine which included golf and skiing. My experience of these two sports, as a complete beginner, convinced me more than ever of the value of Inner Game theory and practice.

It is these principles that I have adapted for riding and the results have been very exciting, not only in the sphere of riding but in a way that is applicable to life in general. For me, it is the link between riding technique and ways of looking at my life that has been the most radical shift of all, because the absorption of information is changed from being an external process to being an internal one. The pupils are helped to discover what they need from their own inner resources, rather than purely from an external instructor. They are no longer simply passive receptors but, instead, take up the search for individual knowledge and, with their coach's help, discover that they not only believe what they find in their heads, but know it in their bones as well. This deep knowledge is far more convincing and far more effective than the rote learning which is the hallmark of much teaching today.

1 Looking at What Helps and Hinders Learning

I wonder what your earliest memories of learning are. Maybe you cannot remember the process at all, yet childhood is the time when we assimilate more knowledge in a short time than we ever will again. Moreover, we usually do so with enormous natural spontaneity and enjoyment. It is a time when new impressions and information come pouring in through all our senses.

A child may become totally absorbed with a flower, a spoon or a handful of mud, then after a period of very close inspection they will discard it again. Without any instruction they soon learn to walk, opening up another whole new world to be explored. What happens to this uninhibited openness and intense curiosity? All too soon these wonderful faculties are atrophied by the dos and don'ts of family life, school, religion, profession and society. We learn to conform, to limit our self-expression. Awareness diminishes and we begin to learn intellectually while using our bodies less. We start to encounter criticism, shame, guilt, fear – all of these bring negative responses. It is all too easy to start thinking we are bad or stupid if we are told often enough. A chain reaction begins as our bodies start to react to our thoughts which in turn affect the way we use our bodies.

When we relate these ideas to riding, we encounter another living species who cannot speak our language but can nevertheless read us like a book. Our thoughts repercuss through the horse's body so that, even though we may be oblivious to it, the horse has become an echo-sounder or radar for our emotions. Poor horse, you may think, but, having made the connections, we can begin to realise that positive attitudes, awareness and intuition can produce wonders which will completely change the situation.

Changing the mental habits of years is not as daunting as it may at first sound, but it does involve looking closely at the attitudes which block the true ability so readily demonstrated by an enthusiastic child. We can uncover this enthusiasm and ability once more if we are prepared to look at ourselves clearly and honestly. Like a child, we have to recover the confidence and awareness that we have forgotten.

We can all remember times at school when we were told that we were stupid, or when we were frightened to say that we did not understand. These feelings, and many others like them, come up frequently when I start asking adult pupils about their experiences. Negative comments made by other people only add to the ones you make about yourself, and they get in the way because you have believed them in the past. Destructive criticism never helped anyone to improve performance, be it on a horse or anywhere else. Looking at anxiety in general, as well as in riding, helps to release those inhibitions which obscure who we really are and what we are capable of doing.

The more confidence you have, the more easily you can move towards the goals you have set for yourself and your horse. Natural riding exercises are useful in reducing the negative attitude which overrides ability and which distracts the horse.

Identifying Negative Aspects

It is better to investigate what we are thinking before we ride, than to risk afflicting the horse with our taut body. Discovering our blocks and how to do something about them is an awareness exercise in itself. This will develop from lesson to lesson, replacing the 'I must try harder' syndrome, and the one that goes with it – 'I must remember to do exactly what the instructor has told me'. Both tend only to put a spanner in the works. Thoughts like 'I was never any good at school' can colour your whole life. Just try counting how many negative thoughts pass through your mind in an hour or in a day. The introductory exercise for stress release which looks at worries and helps you to recognise patterns is another step towards being a positive person. Remember, one step starts a journey of a thousand miles or a whole chain of constructive events.

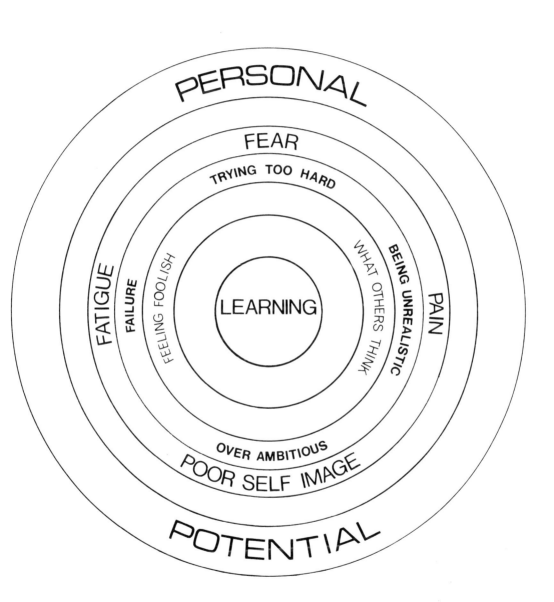

Fig 1 Negative aspects which inhibit learning.

It is well worth trying to achieve a relaxed body almost automatically, for it is only in this state that you recapture the enjoyment of natural learning you had as a child.

The following list has been compiled by students to show the states of mind which limit learning. Many of them occur frequently, and these have been identified with the letter 'F'. Study the list, then make a list of those which you identify with and add any others of which you are aware. The marks given are out of ten and indicate the intensity felt. The physical location of the anxiety is put beside the number, as shown. Try to discover where your anxieties are located.

F	Arthur	—	fear of failing	8	—	breath
	Jane	—	fear of falling off	7	—	tummy
F	Pat	—	fear of looking foolish	6	—	fists
	Madge	—	fear of what others think	7	—	head
					—	not looking
F	Di	—	fear of losing control	8	—	breath
	Jack	—	fear of not hearing	8	—	neck
F	Liz	—	fear of being shouted at	9	—	shoulders
	Zoe	—	fear of the unknown	8	—	shoulders
	Iona	—	fear of not understanding	6	—	forehead

There are many others, but these will suffice to start you off on your own project. Keep your original list so that later you can compare your feelings after doing some breathing exercises, which will be explained later in the chapter.

Identifying Positive Aspects

The negative aspects of ourselves always seem to spring more readily to mind than positive ones, so try this exercise for yourself, listing what you consider are the qualities of a good rider, for example, co-ordination, a good figure, confidence. Make the list as extensive as you can, and then tick the ones which you think apply to you and give yourself marks out of ten, as before. Then compare your list of these positive aspects of yourself with the negative ones to see which is the longest list. This exercise is more helpful when done with other people, but is nevertheless revealing even when you do it on your own.

It is certainly easier to find negative aspects of yourself than positive ones, and it is not surprising to find people who can only list one good thing about themselves for every ten negative things. It is thus high time to change our minds and become realistic about our potential.

Balance is a must for riders, but now its role becomes obvious. Balance starts in the mind. A balanced outlook will help you to have a relaxed body, and the ability to concentrate on the priorities which will bring success. A young mountaineer whom I recently heard being interviewed said, 'You climb your mountain with your mind'. As with mountaineering, good riding also starts with the mind.

Positive Coaching

Traditional coaching generally concentrates on mounted work and does not provide much opportunity for anxiety release exercises. Knowing that such anxieties exist, however, means that the instructor can help to counteract the negativity which each pupil subconsciously contributes. This can be done by creating a sense of security and reassurance within the class, a process which involves deliberately establishing positive relationships and informing the class of the lesson plan. Pupils almost invariably become anxious when they do not know in advance what is going to happen during a lesson.

Relationships are an integral part of a truly instructive lesson. They start with the instructor, whose approach is unconsciously assessed by the group. Coaches therefore learn a lot from watching their group's body language.

This web of interrelationship which develops within a group, is much more complex than it looks on the surface and is one which the instructor can initiate in a positive way by being aware of the implications. The relationships affect everyone who makes up the class or group, and the web that is woven looks like the one shown in Fig 2.

The connections taking place beneath the surface activities are two-way and operate on a positive or negative response. They are as follows:

1. The coach relating to the group.
2. The coach relating to each rider.
3. The coach with each horse.
4. The riders with each other as individuals.
5. The horses with each other as individuals.
6. The rider with his or her horse.
7. Each rider with the other horses.

A negative influence can disrupt a positive atmosphere in a class, as does withdrawing or adding pupils to a group which is already established. The effect of a moody rider or a bad-tempered horse or coach will have been experienced by most pupils at some time in their training. If the instructor pays attention to the following points, any lesson will be more readily assimilated:

• Make sure that all instructions are given clearly.
• Make sure that the instructions are audible to all the members of the group.
• Have realistic expectations about how much can be done and for how long.
• Allow for adequate repetition of each exercise.
• Avoid trying to do too much in the lesson.
• Watch pupils carefully for signs of fatigue and understanding.
• Recognise peaks of concentration; as a rough guide these will happen every twenty minutes for adults, ten minutes for children.
• Remember that the rate of forgetting can be two-thirds of the content of each lesson.
• Remember that distractions can take away 75 per cent of a pupil's attention.
• Remember that each person has a dominant sense which facilitates learning; this is either visual, intellectual or kinetic/physical. The relative importance of

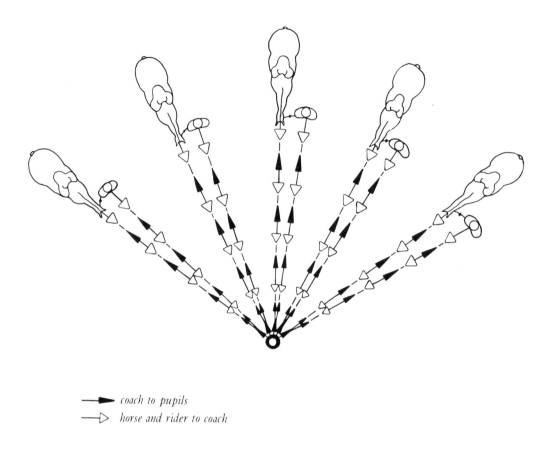

→ *coach to pupils*
⇾ *horse and rider to coach*

Fig 2   Similar relationships connect riders and horses.

these senses can be summed up as: what I hear, I forget; what I see, I believe; what I do, I know.

• Finally, remember that however we help our pupils, there is no teaching without learning taking place.

Here is the story of a lesson which speaks for itself about the way pupils feel when they are in class.

Karen, a teenager, had been promoted to her first horse after outgrowing her pony, and was having considerable difficulty with her new mount. Her horse had had little schooling and was very excit-

able, which resulted in mutual misunderstanding and confrontation. This situation highlighted Karen's long-standing problem of not being deep enough in the saddle and having unsteady hands, both of which continually disturbed the horse. She was asked by the coach to identify the major problems, and, without being judgemental, to pay specific attention to what was happening. Having assessed the situation, she was then asked to choose one of the problems to which she would give her full attention, and work on it until she had something to report.

She chose to notice the feeling of the rein, and went away to carry out the exercise that was given her. It was not long before she came back saying she had had results, but something else had come into the picture. Once more she was given a concentration exercise to look at the problem to which she had given second choice. This difficulty also resolved itself, the picture began to clarify, and the horse settled down.

'What did you discover?' she was asked, to which she readily replied:

'I was too far back in the saddle, and my reins were too long. I was frightened to take a firmer contact, which the horse now likes and so do I.'

'Excellent,' said the coach, 'but supposing I had told you?'

'Oh, I wouldn't have believed you,' was her prompt retort.

She spoke the truth, for no one had been able to help her till then. Internal resistance is often present when we are asked to change, even though we may long to do so. Karen found her way of doing it, made remarkable progress and found confidence as a result. With Karen, words were inadequate. Words alone rarely succeed in real learning, for who can describe accurately what they feel, let alone what someone else should feel. This pupil obviously preferred learning through her kinetic sense, the feeling in her muscles, a feeling which she tracked down quite successfully herself. The amount of tension in this pupil and her horse demonstrated very clearly the major problems. When a tense horse goes to a calmer owner, a new tranquility often seems to develop and its metabolism seems to function more effectively. It develops a confidence and robustness which was not evident before. If this is so

with horses, it must apply to humans as well.

It is not always appreciated how uptight we can become before any event which has any suggestion of ordeal or threat about it. This includes attending lessons when there is an element of the unknown. Here is an example. A coach was waiting for a group of riders to arrive for his course. Everyone had assembled except for one participant. There was a lull in the chattering as everybody waited for something to happen. It was during this lull that the pupil finally arrived, full of apologetic guilt.

This opened up the way for everyone else to sense their own feeling because the coach was able to reassure the class that there would be time to settle down and draw breath before riding. A discussion started where information was gathered about pupils' previous experiences. Because of the tension shown by the new arrival, the coach asked everyone what sort of difficulties they had encountered in order to get away to the course on time. The result was a rush to air individual problems.

On the opening morning there is usually diffidence in answering the initial question, but on this occasion everyone wanted to talk. It was very clear that most people experienced anxiety in a situation which had an unknown threat about it. Two levels of anxiety were obvious: the one that came in with the late pupil and the one that they were looking at in the lesson itself. Time was spent dissolving some of this tension, and the riders were able to disperse with everyone feeling more reassured and relaxed. What emerged was how much effort had been made to organise their families and their businesses, and the worry there had been about traffic or breaking down and being late. This anxiety emerges again and again, and when pupils are allowed to talk they are in a much better frame of mind to ride and to learn. It is important for the coach to take an interest and to ask pupils what sort of journey or what kind of day they have had, how they might be feeling about their lesson, and the steps that can be taken to ease that tension.

Using Your Brain

Having discussed the impact of the mind on the body and how changing your attitude of mind can make a difference to your performance without the usual effort, now is the time to look more closely at how the mind functions. This is a complex subject which scientists are still researching. However, more light has recently been shed on the roles played by the two hemispheres of the brain. Each hemisphere controls its opposite side of the body: the left hemisphere governs the right side of the body and the right one governs the left side. There is also growing evidence to show that the two halves may function in different ways.

In his 'Inner Game' books, Tim Gallwey calls the two separate mental activities that we hear in our heads Self 1 and Self 2, without specifying their precise relationship to the hemispheres. However, the following list shows what is thought to be the roles of the two hemispheres, and is taken from Ronald Shone's book *Creative Visualisation*.

The left hemisphere governs logic, reason, reading, writing, language and analysis. The right is thought to govern recognition, rhythm, creativity, synthesis (seeing things as a whole), dreams,

emotions and feelings, intuition, movement and imagery. A good example of a left brain activity is assessment, while the right brain may produce ideas and pictures of your ideal home or place. A scientific bent may well be left dominated; an artistic one is right dominated. The left brain can become very verbal and self-argumentative at times. Have you noticed dialogues like this: 'I must go and see Ann and James but I haven't time and I don't really want to go, yet I'll feel guilty if I don't make the effort.' Another time you may have a flash of insight and wonder where it came from. Now you know.

Relaxation employs right brain activity which releases the neuro-muscular tension but it is assisted by the left brain which expresses feelings through words helping to create pleasant mental pictures. There seems to be a dominance of one side of the brain or the other, but when they interact in balance you get the best of both of them.

In our civilisation, education tends to be left brain orientated, which often does not give the other half a chance. Our hidden potential may rely on this unused part being elevated to its proper place. Where riding is concerned, with increasing mental poise there is less likelihood of the horse being brainwashed by our human intellectualising.

The complexity of the brain is constantly under review. Debate continues as to what actually happens in the brain, and the full scope of its functions is still a mystery. The right brain/left brain distinction I have outlined is of necessity an overly simple explanation about one theory. An interesting book has been written by Betty Edwards called *Drawing with the Right Side of the Brain*, which contains interesting exercises for exploration. Whether you draw or not, it shows how relaxation and awareness of left and right brain functions can help you to do so, and demonstrates pertinent parallels in many activities, perhaps explaining why riders often have this artistic ability.

It is, after all, this intuitive side of ourselves we need to recognise and trust. It is this faculty which helps us tune in to the horse and develop better understanding.

A pupil's answers to the following questions, which are used to clarify progress made, may illustrate how the rider finds out about himself and his relationship to the horse and even his children. Pupils who complete these questions find the process helpful in clarifying their experience.

Q.   Have you been coached in any skill or sport before?
A.   Yes, I've been coached in rugby and sailing.

Q.   What made you want to ride?
A.   To overcome a lifelong fear of horses.

Q.   What difference did you notice with this coaching technique?
A.   There is a more sensitive and relaxed approach to learning, by guidance and encouragement, rather than direct command and repetition of 'failed' exercises.

Q.   What did you feel at the beginning about the horse?
A.   I was still very unsure that riding was for me, and unsure of my ability. I was decidedly nervous of the horse itself. Fortunately, I had a great deal of faith in the coach.

Q.   What were your feelings at the end about the horse, the coach and riding in general?
A.   I had a tremendous feeling of satisfaction at having gained a measure of co-operation with the horse, and had more than achieved my initial aims. I felt totally at home with the horse. The coach showed exemplary patience, teaching by example and encouragement, and only pulling me up if I was likely to cause discomfort, teach the horse bad habits or put it in a position where I was asking it to do the impractical or impossible. Riding has become an enjoyable pastime for me and I intend to continue and improve if I can.

Q.   Did you have any particular difficulties?
A.   I had no difficulty with the horse, as she was gentle and generally co-operative. Once my nervousness faded I became so absorbed that I had little difficulty with myself, and certainly had no difficulty with the coach. The 'Inner Game' methods initially seemed a bit strange, but I found that being asked what I would like to achieve each day helped me to concentrate and learn.

Q.   Were you ever fatigued?
A.   Just a bit at the beginning, in the inner thigh muscles.

Q.   What experience was most useful to you?
A.   Learning to co-operate with the horse.

Q.   Was the experience useful to you in other situations?
A.   I find that the experience has been useful in training my working dogs and also with my children. Rather than 'Don't do that' I now say 'Perhaps if you tried this...'. It's difficult to put into words.

19

Q. Was it worth getting up early every morning?

A. It was well worth getting up earlier every morning, starting the day relaxed and with a sense of achievement.

Q. Would you have learnt more easily with orthodox instruction?

A. Starting as I did with a fear of horses, I don't think I would have learnt at all with orthodox instruction. When you are told 'do' and 'don't', you tense up and try to do exactly as you're being instructed. If I had been tense I would not have been able to feel and respond to the horse, and would probably have ended up dispirited and sore, not learning anything, and not enjoying riding at all.

Goals

Goals add a self-motivating boost to your riding progress, providing they are set with clarity. Vague and unrealistic goals will only lead to disappointment, so it is well worth giving some thought to what you really want to achieve. The word 'want' in itself is an impetus. If you want to do something, you are likely to succeed, whereas 'wishing' has a wistful connotation and is not so effective.

When pupils are asked why they ride and what they enjoy, there is often a pause while the question is considered. It is not so readily answered as you might think. Try it for yourself or on a friend or a child. We are not always clear about the reasons which motivate us.

A goal is a target and needs to be realistic and well defined. When you do this defining process, an internal self-correcting mechanism operates to keep you on course using negative feedback.

For example, if your body weight is behind the horse's movement you will feel uncomfortable and want to do something about it. This is how the self-guided torpedo is kept on course by a corrective device in its rudder. If your horse is resisting, ask yourself what is in the way, what is not working. The answer may well be in the way you respond to the question 'Are you trying to do anything in particular?' If you respond readily in the affirmative, you will have acknowledged the source of difficulty which has arisen as a result of your own resistance when you changed from going with events, to trying to maintain them. This is an example of resistance indicating being off course through the negative feedback produced by the horse.

The temptation to try to make something happen can arise at all stages of training and, as the rider advances and greater expertise is expected of horse and rider, so does the need to notice the signs which indicate discrepancies and to accept them thankfully. When you understand your own reactions it is easier to adjust your sights when off target.

It is, however, important to set your target within reach because nothing is more disheartening than an unrealistic range, which leaves the feeling of always falling short of it, and which will also occur if you become too obsessed with end results.

Try setting up goals for yourself, by putting them into long-, mid- or short-term spans, so that they form stepping stones which lead to success. As an example, you might choose a long-term goal of being able to produce your dressage horse at medium test level or compete with your show-jumper in fox-hunter competitions. A mid-term goal, on the other hand, will bridge the gap by aiming at novice-level dressage and novice show-jumping competitions. The same idea relates to goals within lessons or daily practice which then become your short-term aims.

The main points to remember in setting successful targets are: to define them visually, specify the time span and keep them realistic. Then once you have set them, devote your full attention to the process which will eventually take you to them.

A short-term example of a goal-orientated lesson could be choosing to make smooth transitions into and out of canter. This involves deciding how much improvement would satisfy you in the available time and how many improved transitions you would expect the horse to perform. Ask these questions:

QUESTION
1. What is my goal?
2. How committed do I feel?
3. What time is available?
4. How much improvement do I want?
5. How many improved responses from the horse?
6. Is this goal realistic?

ANSWER
1. Smooth canter transitions
2. 90 per cent
3. 45 minutes
4. 40 per cent
5. 5 out of 10
6. Yes

Each answer increases your sense of commitment, almost subconsciously. You can now forget the goal and carry on with your riding, with just an odd check to see if you are moving towards it. Being specific in this way makes your target more attainable, whatever it is you want to accomplish.

Visualising your goal in detail also increases the chance of achievement. You can do it while you rest your horse during schooling, or in any spare moments you have, the most effective time being when you wake first thing or just before falling asleep. Again, for it to work you need to create a detailed picture of yourself and your horse in a beautiful arena, performing effortlessly, filling in details of background and weather to make your picture more real. The effect of these mental exercises may not show for three weeks or so, though results have often been noticed within a week, certainly enough to make you feel that they are worth doing.

Do not become over-anxious about the goal you set. You can forget it while you work. Goals tend to look after themselves if you keep your attention in the present. Learn to trust this subconscious self-righting mechanism and enjoy your riding more.

To sum up this chapter on learning, there are three ways of assimilating knowledge. The first way of learning is from the teacher, who is the obvious authority, providing information and putting the pupil in the role of the accepter of it. The second way is through the discovery of a self-awareness which utilises the senses and is gained through the guidance of the coach. The coach becomes a facilitator to help pupils gain knowledge from within, through a process of active participation. The third way of learning is through a function called latent learning. This takes place when the pupil is at rest, and is more likely to follow any session that ended on a good note. This function can also affect the horse, as well as other animals. It can be recognised when marked progress appears without intervening practice, and it often appears to happen spontaneously, sometimes after a considerable period of time. The process of latent learning can be stimulated by using relaxation and visualisation techniques between lessons.

Learning to improve while you sleep may seem a fanciful idea, but it is possible if you practise regularly and make good use of any time available. The learning activities do not involve any effort except the need to set aside five or ten minutes, once or twice a day.

Here is an exercise that you can practise whenever you have time. It is important to practise regularly for a short time, once a day at least, in order for it to be effective. If you can manage to do it twice a day, then you will increase its effect.

Lie down on your back, or sit in a chair or even on your horse, but be comfortable. Put a hand on your diaphragm and, as you breath, try and push it out. As you get used to this different sensation when inhaling, notice the rhythm of your breathing. Let it be natural and easy, breathing in and out, five or six times to begin with. Most people breathe inefficiently and thus deprive their body and

brain of oxygen, while a delayed exchange of carbon dioxide is detrimental to well-being and stamina. By focusing the attention lower down your body, the lungs have a chance to fill up more easily.

Avoid forcing the breath – just let it happen and notice what it feels like. Do it whenever you have a moment to spare, and you will soon begin to breathe more easily without trying. As you breathe out, stay calm. This word alone, 'calm', can produce a physical response in time, so that when you most need to relax it will become spontaneous. The effect will depend upon how regularly you practise this simple exercise.

Here is another exercise to improve your breathing, awareness and relaxation. Stand with your arms at your side. Quietly raise them, inhaling slowly, until they touch above your head. Slowly lower your arms and exhale. Repeat this five or six times, noticing the feeling of lifting up on the in-breath and letting go on the out-breath. Do this twice a day. Later on, you can rise up on your toes as you inhale and come down as you exhale, extending the repetitions to increase control. It is possible to do this on a horse which will stand safely, or if someone is available to hold it, but proceed very quietly. Notice the way it affects your weight in the saddle and the muscles in your arms.

2 The Rider

Reducing Resistance

The first chapter explained how we unwittingly erect our own self-limiting barriers to learning, and how when we confront them by trying too hard we are faced with a resistance in our muscles. Thoughts like 'I must do better' or 'I must make myself canter' are indicative of this conflict and the tension which accompanies it before we are even in the saddle. It conjures up the body language of stiffness and grim determination – gritting the teeth and clenching the fists.

Pupils sometimes arrive for lessons spinning like tops with the external pressures of trying to be on time, and their internal anxieties about their riding. Feeling this uptight is not a conducive state in which to start riding because of the physical inhibitions it imposes. When this happens, the centre of gravity changes, the shoulders are hunched and breathing is shallow, all of which brings on imbalance in our posture.

This chapter is about the art of non-doing. Non-doing is about putting to one side the usual list of instructions of all the things that pupils should be doing. Instead, they are helped to gather their thoughts and focus their attention on significant physical changes, using exercises which concentrate their interest on what is actually happening. When they do this, awareness increases and relaxation is able to take place. Then and only then is the body free to find its natural balance without resistance getting in the way.

Try this next exercise as an example of visualisation, helping you to 'let go'. It can be done sitting in a chair, or even on your horse. Imagine you are a spinning-top gradually slowing down until you become a triangle, pointing downwards with the flat edge uppermost. When you can see this, add another triangle, point to point, under the one you have in your mind, so that the two together form an egg-timer or hour glass. Now let your busy thoughts and anxieties trickle through into the bottom triangle, which has become a pyramid. As your thoughts fall to the bottom of the pyramid, they become sand warmed by the sun. Go into this pyramid and sit quietly in the warmth, stillness and security. Concentrate on the warmth in your abdomen and say slowly, two or three times, 'I am calm and relaxed'. Try to sense the physical letting go of your limbs, and notice your breathing. When you feel more tranquil, you are ready to start your practical work. Practising this technique, at least twice a day, can produce results within a week. For deeper calmness you will probably need to persist for at least a month.

Eventually, just picturing a pyramid or the word 'calm' will be all that is required to produce calmness in times of stress or crisis. You can, of course, create your own calming scenes, and the more often you do this, the more vivid they will become. Remember to picture as many details as you can to make them even more useful in your self-programming. The most impressionable time is just before you go to sleep or when you wake in the morning when it can make a difference to your whole day, not only to your riding.

Preparing yourself before you ride, using this exercise or simply by monitoring your breathing, is well worthwhile. It centres your thinking and helps you to be aware of your body. Understanding how anxiety affects you physically is the first step towards relaxation, which is the vital factor underlying balance. Riding without resistance requires an inner knowing as much as external information. The vital information you need is already within you, and it is this concept which will help you to unlock the door to your true potential.

The spinning-top analogy illustrates how we see and use time. Few people would deny feeling a shortage of time, and in our haste to keep to our schedule we tend to live in a permanent future. This perception constantly influences the extent of our awareness. Today, time is money, and time is at a premium. Yet there is also a sense of wasting the time we have by not concentrating on the present. We waste time because we lose awareness of the true experience of living, whatever the gain may be. Awareness begins *here* and *now*, not yesterday or tomorrow. By setting a goal and then putting it aside, you can turn to the present process with all your attention and interest and, by reducing anxiety about the results, you will find that you have achieved them more easily and with more enjoyment.

Using Your Senses

Clearing your mind and calming down before you ride is the first priority and you can do it either before you get on the horse or in the saddle. You may choose to use the spinning-top analogy. Alternatively, you can put your unwanted thoughts and anxieties in an imaginary dustbin or make a bonfire of them, or listen to your breathing for a few minutes

and notice the rhythm. There are other ways of becoming calm which can be added to this list and you will find more suggestions as you read through the chapters of this book, and as you become more creative yourself.

Make a habit of observing and assessing how uptight you feel, for whatever reason, and then become more specific by assessing it on a percentage basis. Your internal computer needs facts. When you have had a few minutes to let go, re-evaluate the tension after you have done your relaxation exercise. Notice especially if the physical symptoms have changed. We all tighten different areas of our bodies when we feel under pressure: we hold our breath; we hunch our shoulders; we set our jaws and tighten our

Fig 3   This photograph shows how our bodies affect the horse.

Fig 4   *A tense rider and horse – how the horse reflects our bodies.*

Fig 5   *A relaxed rider and horse.*

abdomens. By breathing quietly, with your mind on the pyramid, you will encourage a more centred feeling. When sitting on the horse, visualise the pyramid once more, feel centred, and secure in your saddle. By becoming more composed you give the horse a better deal, too. The horse literally feels the way you think and, in turn, reflects your anxiety with its resistance.

Resilient confidence can be developed by using the techniques which are given in this book. Let us look again at the main things we have learnt so far.

• Develop your sensory capacity by using as many of your senses as possible: hearing, seeing, touching, doing – even smelling.
• Increase your range of discovery by reducing the fear of being right or wrong, correct or incorrect.
• Be prepared to explore your experiences; this increases the information to which your body and mind can respond, and helps you in the development of your awareness.
• Learn to listen to your horse and to understand its body language.
• Stay in the present.
• Concentrate on one thing at a time.
• Above all, avoid trying too hard to get it right, and feeling a sense of failure when you do not succeed.

Communication and Body Language

Being aware of your body language will lead to better understanding between you and your horse. Horses are often confused by inadvertent contradictions, such as when a conscious signal is counter-

manded by a subconscious one. When both are in unison, the horse has a much better chance of understanding you. Such a conflicting message might be observed when someone says 'Yes' yet shakes the head negatively, without realising – this happens more often than you think. You might ask yourself, like the horse, which is the true answer. Remember that it is your body language which never lies; the horse knows this.

The horse's dilemma is increased when you say one thing with your riding aids and oppose it with what you really want to do through your body language. To become aware of what you say unconsciously with your body is not easy, because ingrained habits blur your sensory capacity, yet it is this sensitivity which can unlock true ability; it can extend your vocabulary for fuller communication, not only with the horse, but with other people, too.

The sequence which will open up new awareness before you ride is this:

1. Gather your thoughts and anxieties without feeling guilty. Admit, either verbally or to yourself, exactly how you feel.
2. Discard these thoughts and anxieties by symbolically throwing down your whip (providing it does not frighten your horse). Alternatively, you can imagine yourself putting these thoughts in a black box and burying it, or you can burn them on a bonfire or tie them to a balloon and watch them fly away.
3. Notice physical tenseness, both before you think of the imagery and after. Assess it on a percentage basis, so that you know exactly how it feels. Perhaps it is 80 per cent to begin with and comes down to 60 per cent.

4. Do this assessment with your anxiety level, too.

5. Breathe quietly for a few minutes.

6. Visualise the spinning-top turning into a pyramid while you sit calmly within.

7. Now reassess both percentages. This should indicate a reduction in both mental and physical tension.

This routine will help you to gather information from physical changes as you become more tuned in to your thought patterns and physical reactions. The feedback from imagery and breathing highlights subtle differences too. Listening to your body will make it easier to listen to the horse. Assessing exactly how you feel gives you a reliable reference point and informs your subconscious mind of precise facts. Being able to exert some control and influence over such complex systems can improve your riding by reducing resistance, the resistance so often encountered when riding and training horses.

The Detective

The role you are evolving for yourself as a rider might be likened to that of a detective. The detective is constantly scrutinising the situation for clues in both your own and your horse's mind and body. The symptoms which arise usually have their source elsewhere, and when a problem does not resolve itself then you can be sure you have not found the root cause. If the first trail of clues is abortive, you will need to choose another focus of attention, approaching it from a different angle in the attempt to reveal the real reason for the symptom. In traditional riding training, the constant criticism of a difficulty tends to inhibit the discovery of the trigger point, which is often far removed from the immediate evidence. Constant reminders and constant effort are proof of an unresolved difficulty. It is here that detective riders come into their own, with the help of a coach, a friend or through their own awakening. Here is how one pupil tracked down her own problem.

Sally had always had a problem with her shoulders, a problem which she had been unable to modify however hard she tried and however often she was told. This left her feeling very defeated. She was asked by the coach to sit comfortably, rather than correctly, and then to ride her horse at the 'walk' until she could pin-point any particular sensation that caught her attention. When she came back she said in a surprised voice, 'It's my hips where I feel the discomfort.' Sally's coach suggested an awareness exercise for her hips, which she went away and investigated. As she did this the shoulders gradually improved, until she began to look quite impressive on her horse. The audience who had come in to watch Sally's lesson said that they had never seen her ride so well.

After the lesson Sally discussed what had happened. She said that her hips were now much more comfortable, and she had forgotten about her shoulders altogether. She now felt a new poise in her posture.

Sally's experience demonstrates the detective at work, exploring other clues that might lie beneath the persistent problem. In discovering that the real difficulty lay lower down in her body, Sally's shoulders came naturally into balance and were more relaxed.

Fig 6   A round shoulders problem.

Fig 7   Rider's reaction to being told to sit up.

Fig 8   Rider's reaction to 'thinking tall'.

The rider who looks at a problem as a whole is much more likely to find the real source of the trouble and, by paying attention to it, can solve other problems as well as the major one, thus improving overall performance. Your coach can often act as a sounding-board for you, helping you to answer the important questions that you are asking yourself. The feedback which your answers contribute may surprise you both.

When new ideas are presented to pupils, a dismounted briefing process is important. It is valuable before all lessons, because it helps to defuse the apprehension which builds up before an unknown situation. Any change in the format of the lesson makes it a new situation, and a pre-ride explanation of the general plan of action is reassuring. These changes can be given more attention when pupils are dismounted. Many pupils admit that not knowing what is going to happen can make them apprehensive. This is completely understandable, and the relief experienced when an explanation is given is sensed not only by the rider but also by the horse. Here is one way of organising a lesson:

1.   Questions and answers to help everyone to gather their thoughts and reflect on their feelings.
2.   An assurance that the lesson will be non-judgemental. This will bring the confidence to investigate, assess and create individual ways of doing exercises which will hold the pupil's interest and attention. It also enables relaxation to

take place and natural alignment to come about effortlessly.

The body really does know how to perform if we can only trust it. It is lack of faith in ourselves that causes unwanted tension. Difficulties arise when riders try too hard to improve. The question 'What are you trying to do?' helps them to pause and recognise what is happening. This can help at all levels of training, but especially where demands are more complex and standards higher.

The ideal learning situation provides a trained horse for each novice rider, so that control and balance can develop without distractions. In the same way, a horse that is learning to be ridden needs an experienced rider who can train it. Yet there are still many occasions when both horse and rider seem to be struggling along together, very much like the blind leading the blind, both lacking the training they need to find mutual balance and some degree of co-operation.

Providing there is no threat to safety in this all too common predicament, it is surprising how much progress is possible if resistance in the form of tension can be minimised. It is a question of the rider taking one step at a time towards an awareness of himself or herself and the horse, keeping the attention on what seems important and remembering to keep an eye on any tendency to increase the effort involved. Pupils find themselves taking more time to think and feel their way towards confidence in themselves and their horses, while enjoying a new sense of time which this appears to give them. Not being in a hurry is a novel sensation for most riders, and the horse's positive response can be very rewarding.

Introducing the Horse

In normal life, when we meet each other, certain rituals take place as we make signs of recognition and sum one another up on the basis of our aquaintanceship. When we encounter another person, we also recognise unconsciously the reactions that are taking place, and the same applies when we meet our horses.

On occasions, when we meet one another, the impressions are sometimes so casual that they could be an affront, and at others so effusive that they impinge on our personal space. How then do we meet the horse we are about to ride? Does it warrant a friendly greeting before we are in the saddle?

In the first chapter, reference was made to the importance of the relationships which develop between people, between animals, and between animals and people. The point being made was that a positive attitude makes a constructive impact. Whatever horse you are riding, it deserves a few minutes of welcome before you start a session together.

Your preliminary observations should cover the fitting and condition of the saddlery. If you do not know how this should be done, the sooner you learn the better. Your safety may well depend on this knowledge. There is more to the fitting of saddles and bridles than meets the casual eye, and guide-lines do not always cover the less obvious aspects. Knowledge comes through experience rather than from books, for nothing replaces the practical experience of handling saddlery and seeing bridles and saddles fitted on different horses. Further details are given in Chapter 4, page 70.

In your inspection, include the general appearance and attitude of the horse you

Fig 9   Making friends.

are riding, even if it belongs to you. If it is yours, minor discrepancies may be noticed at once. If the horse is a borrowed or hired mount, your first general impression may hold clues to its personality, as well as to its condition.

The mounting preparation, including the checking of girths and stirrup leathers, may seem long-winded, but its psychological importance as well as its practical usefulness makes it well worthwhile. Before you mount, make time to stop and stare, to consider the horse you are going to ride. Give the horse time to do the same. Relationships are two-way and start at this point.

The emphasis on awareness in this chapter is as much for the horse's benefit as for yours, because it cannot speak for itself. Although many books describe the mounting procedure very clearly from the rider's point of view, the vulnerability of the horse is not so adequately stressed.

The Way to Mount

It is the horse that receives the rider's weight on its back, so how we arrive there is extremely important, as is the correct fitting of the saddle on which you sit. More horses than can be imagined have been damaged by uncoordinated mounting, and once the pattern of discomfort or pain is imprinted on the horse's memory, it will take evasive action. This can compound an injury, which may become chronic.

Mounting needs to be done with great care at all times, because horses may suffer for years without it being noticed. Begin by noticing how your horse reacts to your arrival in the saddle. This will tell you at once whether you are really paying attention, because apprehension may cause it to dip its back, and it may be uneasy about standing still. When the horse stands with its back hollow in defence and its hind legs pushed out behind, it is under considerable strain. This will also show when it is asked to move forward, which it will do with difficulty. When these symptoms are commented upon by the coach, replies like the following are common: 'I've never noticed before'; 'Oh, he always does that'; 'He will never stand still'; 'He is disobedient'; 'He has a cold back'.

When the horse's back is inspected, it is often found to be suffering from tenderness. When this symptom arises, it is important to make a thorough investigation and, if necessary obtain veterinary advice. Another cause of damage is when the rider pulls the back of the saddle across the spine and sits down on it before it has time to spring back into place. This, too, causes bruising of the spine which, if severe, requires a considerable period of rest to heal.

With these considerations in mind, together with the physical difficulty of mounting which some riders encounter, it is understandably a manoeuvre which requires practice and care. Riders can suffer from a sense of panic when it comes to mounting. This tempts them to perform it too quickly, before the horse moves. We must therefore consider the options which can change your sense of inadequacy and the horse's apprehension about the imminent onslaught to a sense of mutual confidence. The ability to mount your horse single-handed is of course the target, but horses, even when trained, do not always oblige by standing still. When the horse does not stand still it is important to make sure that its back is not sore and to assess what distraction may be causing it to move about. Perhaps it is a lack of training or a fear of being separated from its friends. It is no use blaming yourself if the horse is making conditions impossible and the need for assistance imperative.

If the horse is in need of training, it will take time to teach it basic obedience. The only other alternative is to find someone to help you by holding the horse. When the horse is too large, the obvious solution is to mount off a block or find someone who can give you a leg up.

Mounting from a block can be used more frequently than you might think. For some reason, using this method for mounting too often seems to be an admission of failure. It is, however, extremely practical. It not only saves the horse's back and the saddle-tree, but also the rider's breeches. It also has the added advantage of demanding obedience from the horse in standing by the block while you get on, which, without the association of discomfort when you do so, it is much more likely to do. To know the horse is willing to stand quietly by any available object which enables you to get on its back is extremely useful, especially in the hunting field.

The rider for whom lack of spring and co-ordination makes mounting from the ground difficult may well find a poise they have never before discovered, particularly in the last stage of mounting from the block. By stepping comfortably into the stirrup in balance, they can find the control which was previously lacking. Familiarity with this last phase of mounting leads to confidence and kinetic experience which, in time, may make mounting from the ground a real possibility.

Having checked that the saddle and bridle fit comfortably, take up the girth but do this as gently as possible to prevent the horse becoming irritated. Many horses have become resentful about this being done, owing to roughness in the past. Biting and kicking are the ways in which they express discomfort, together with blowing out their belly to resist tightness. When they do this, they are in fact inhaling and holding their breath, which they can do with considerable efficiency. When they release it the girth can be dangerously slack. Horses often learn to do this early on in their training. How would you like rough treatment every time something was tightened around your waist? Remember that a horse who is stabled may spend the winter being ridden out with a saddle held in place by a tight girth and, when at rest, in a rug with a tight roller. Anyone who has tried to test the tension of the latter when the horse is lying down will realise how uncomfortable the pressure can be. When this impinges on the withers, serious damage can be inflicted on this vulnerable area. Other pressure points are involved where rugs are concerned – around the horse's shoulders, and around the hind legs where the straps go which keep New Zealand rugs in place.

When the girth has been tightened, the next step is to release the stirrup irons. Dragging them down the leather, over the ridge which the stirrup iron makes, damages the leather and makes a sharp snapping sound which can frighten young horses. It is also more effort pulling against resistance. By raising the end of the stirrup leather with your spare hand, you can guide it down quietly, quickly and with ease.

Some riders tend to be in too much of a

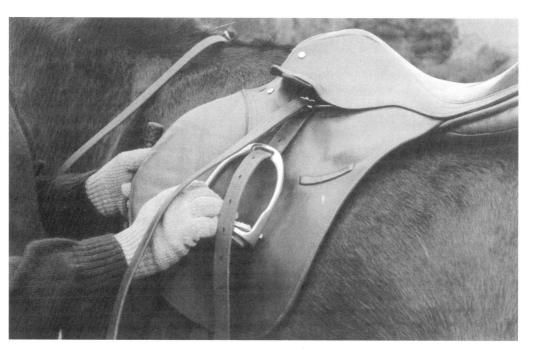

Fig 10   Dragging the stirrup iron down the leather.

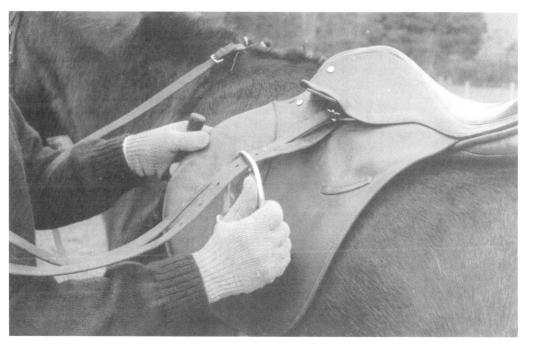

Fig 11   Easing it down.

hurry to bother checking the length they are going to require and, as a result, may need to make considerable alterations in the saddle, making it not only more difficult for them but more uncomfortable for the horse.

There are times when the left leather may need to be longer for mounting purposes, but knowing exactly how much it has been lowered means that it can quickly be levelled once you are mounted. Whether you need to lower your leather or not, do make sure that before you do so both stirrups look even when the horse is standing square and that the saddle is central.

When you have mounted and are making final adjustments, try to reduce your movements to the minimum to avoid displacing the saddle, which may bruise the horse's spine.

When you mount, you should try to pick up the off stirrup iron without using your hand or looking down. Once this is done, there should be no further need to remove your feet to make adjustments. To accomplish this your ankles need to be supple, and practice is necessary to know what to do when you are on the move and inadvertently lose your stirrups. No one will wait in the hunting field, nor will you want to stop in the middle of a show-jumping round.

Here is a check-list of the things worth paying attention to before and during mounting:

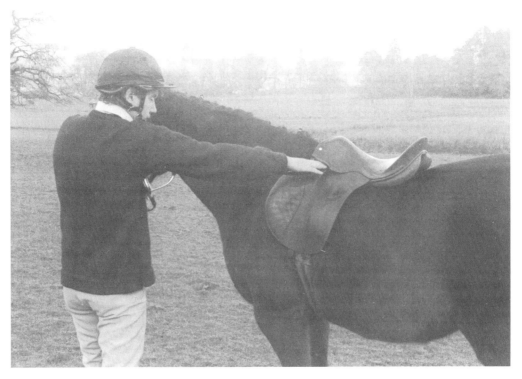

Fig 12   *Measuring the length of the stirrup leather.*

1. Check your saddlery and the horse, using this time to make friends with the horse.

2. Adjust the girth tactfully before attending to the stirrup leathers.

3. Release the stirrup irons. You can check the length by putting your fingertips on the bar of the saddle and bringing the iron down to your armpit. The accuracy of this will depend on the length of your arm, and can be confirmed after dismounting at the end of the ride.

4. Pick up your reins with an even contact which controls the horse. Should it persist in moving, tighten the offside rein so that the horse's hindquarters move towards you, rather than away leaving you hopping on one leg. Then put your left hand and the reins on the withers. Being careless about the reins teaches your horse to evade you because it becomes uncomfortable. Put your whip down the near shoulder to save poking out the eye of an assistant on the offside. It is then ready in your left hand when you move off, not diagonally down the opposite shoulder.

5. Stand beside your horse, your left shoulder against his, facing towards the quarters.

6. Put your left foot fully into the stirrup, which you have turned towards you by catching the far side of the iron. Avoid pushing the horse with your toe, then hop round and face the saddle with your left knee pushed into it. You are

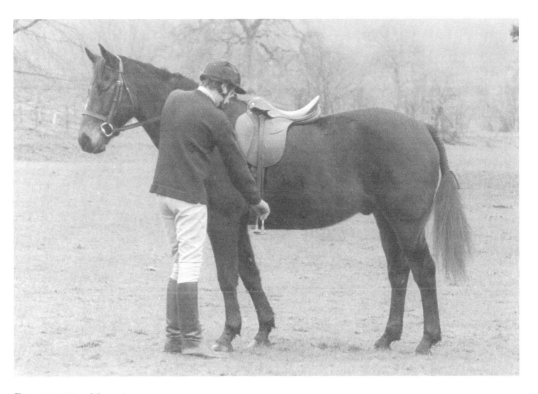

Figs 13–18   Mounting sequence.

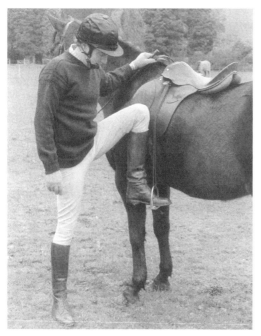

Fig 14.

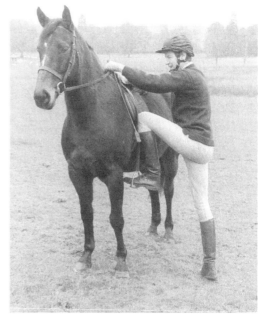

Fig 15.

Fig 16.

Fig 17.

38

Fig 18.

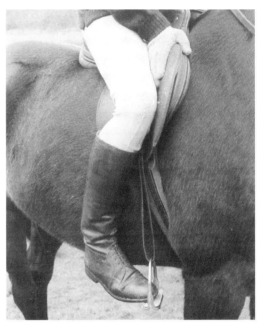

Fig 19 Correct method of putting the foot in the stirrup iron.

now facing the saddle.

7. Put your right hand on the waist or middle of the saddle and, if possible, on the pommel, though this is more difficult. Do not use the cantle.

8. Your left knee will now be pushed against the saddle, while you will be poised to spring off your right leg. As you do so, think of your left knee straightening as your body is lifted off the ground. This adds extra thrust to the manoeuvre and makes it easier for you.

9. Try to lift your body in balance so that you can pause in an upright position before bringing your right leg over and sitting down in the saddle. This will ensure that you control the arrival of your weight on the horse's back.

10. Take up the stirrup iron on the offside without using your hands or looking down and, having done so, check your girth for appropriate security.

11. Make further adjustments without

Fig 20 Incorrect method, using the hand.

Fig 21 *Incorrect way to adjust girth with foot out of stirrup iron.*

Fig 22 *Correct way to adjust girth with foot in stirrup iron.*

shifting your body from side to side, displacing the saddle and making the horse uncomfortable. Remember that once your feet are in the stirrups, there should be no need to take them out for future adjustments. This complicates a simple action and exposes you to insecurity, especially if you take one foot out and not the other. It also makes the sense of evenness in the length of your leathers more difficult to assess. You will need to practise doing this so that you are able to recover a stirrup iron while on the move and at any pace, because it is not always possible to stop and sort yourself out.

These directions on how to mount may seem overcomplicated but, by paying attention to them, you will find the procedure recommended is safe and practical and protects the horse from painful experiences and associations.

There is no disgrace in accepting one's

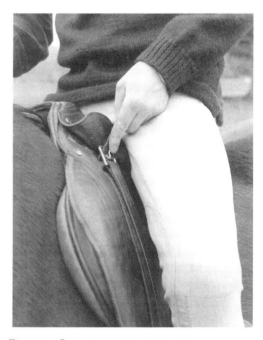

Fig 23 *Correct way to adjust stirrup leather. Notice position of the hand to manipulate the buckle.*

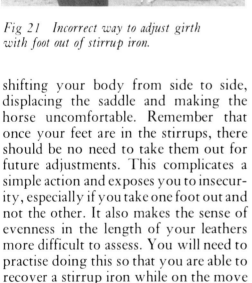

Fig 24   Incorrect dismount.

Fig 25   Correct dismount.

limitations in this respect. We are not all born with the gymnastic ability which mounting demands. The priority is to reach the saddle with the minimum of discomfort for you and the horse.

In the Saddle

Once in the saddle, settle yourself comfortably rather than 'correctly', taking time to find out what comfort really means for you. When you have done this, do the following relaxation exercise to help you feel in balance. Check for tenseness in your body in this order: neck, jaw, shoulders, arms, elbows, wrists,

hands and fingers, breathing, abdomen, seat muscles, thighs, knees, ankles and toes. Spend a minute or two noticing each of these areas in turn. Move them gently, to become aware of them. Gradually become centred in the pyramid that you visualised earlier. Make the shape of the pyramid to suit you as you sit firm and relaxed in the saddle. Your head is in the apex feeling tall, and you are sitting on the base, feeling calm and secure. With your eyes either open or shut, repeat two or three times, 'I'm calm and comfortable'. Be aware of your connections with the horse – seat, legs, hands and mind, and ask yourself which you can sense the most. Is there anything else that makes

Fig 26 Ready to ride.

you aware of your own body? What do you sense about your horse as you sit quietly waiting to start your schooling session?

Whatever you feel to be most important will most likely be the first focal point of attention and you can recheck this once you are on the move, when you will be given one of the awareness exercises to help you to improve your balance.

Balance, which is the hallmark of the successful performer, can be achieved through awareness and relaxation. This short-circuits the effort of trying to sit correctly. One approach can release undue tension and another produce it, and it is these two options which you are now about to explore, giving you the chance to form your own conclusions.

Natural alignment happens without making the body conform to a particular pattern, or trying to remember a fixed string of instructions. Being your own detective gives your intuition a chance to unlock your true ability. The following chapter explains how you can find the keys to do this.

3 Games

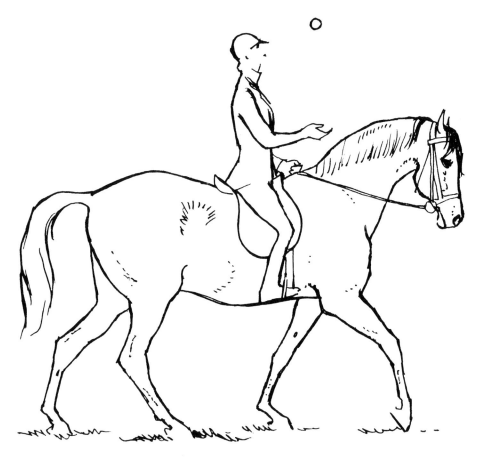

The title of this chapter may arouse some curiosity, so it merits an explanation. The word Games has been chosen as a heading for the techniques and teaching aids used in natural riding lessons. The object of the games is to encourage pupils to utilise as many of their senses as possible. Some of them require visual awareness, others the physical sensing we call 'feel' in riding. Often both are employed simultaneously. Listening 'games' also increase the rider's general awareness. It is not always possible when you are in the saddle to see what is happening, and the games provide useful evidence. The games have proved their worth, helping riders to identify problems and find solutions without becoming dependent on them.

Asking Questions

Questions and answers play a significant part of this mounted programme, together with awareness games and relaxation exercises. These techniques help to reduce the 'spinning-top' state of mind by focusing your attention on your answer.

Pausing to gather your busy thoughts is enough to relieve some of the mental and physical tenseness. It illustrates the activities of the two voices you often hear in your head, which Tim Gallwey identifies as a dialogue, in moments of indecision and when you are trying to do something well and you fail. Self 1, the conscious analytical mind, can be a harsh critic, while occupying the stage to the exclusion of Self 2. Self 2, who has access to your subconscious and influences the body, takes a back seat in this situation and its valuable contribution to what we really need is ignored.

The questions help to control Self 1's distracting activities by focusing the attention on the answer. While this is being reflected upon, Self 2 surfaces with accurate information about how you really feel deep down and what you genuinely want to do. Riders are often surprised at the clarity of their answers, when Self 1 has stopped worrying about not knowing, looking foolish in front of others and giving the wrong answer. The body begins to relax when Self 1 relinquishes some of its control and is retrained to gather facts and not fantasies. When this happens, riders find their own innate information, and the discovery replaces the usual single-track method of instruction.

Being told what to do is not always constructive because words can be misinterpreted and no one can adequately describe their individual experiences. Telling pupils what to do can imply criticism and judgement. Questions, on the other hand, encourage an exchange of information which often reveals the source of chronic problems and misunderstandings.

Initially, this technique can feel inhibiting for some pupils because questioning has overtones of school-like authority, where right and wrong answers could make or mar the day. Overcoming this initial hurdle, however, leaves the riders free to discuss how they feel and what they want to do, which results in relaxed progress.

Finding Your Balance

When describing balance, it is important to remember that you cannot isolate the physical components from the mental and emotional ones. All three are involved when the rider is using his or her senses to the full.

The most meaningful experience of balance for a rider is to sit bareback on a safe and confortable horse. Without the impediment of the saddle, the rider's body falls naturally into balance, and the overall awareness is of warmth.

Riders and horses benefit from this mutual contact, both becoming pleasantly aware of each other's bodies. It is important to understand that this experience is not a dubious activity which precludes safety considerations, because any sense of insecurity defeats the purpose of the exercise. It is sufficient simply to sit on the horse while it stands still, relating the feeling of the horse's back and rib-cage to your body. It may be appropriate to move into a walk, at other times a slow jog, but control of the horse must be the priority. So much depends on the reliability and comfort of your horse, and it should be wearing

Fig 27   Direct contact with the horse.   *Fig 28   Adapting to the saddle.*

a neck strap. The importance of this sensation can influence the rider's position even when the saddle is reintroduced.

This introduction to the feel of balance, of being 'over your base', is not always possible in the learning situation, but when it is, replacing the saddle should be done in stages. First it should be introduced without the stirrups, and secondly with them, but without disturbing the natural alignment of the upper body and legs. It is not always safe to ride without stirrups, but when it is, even if only in walk or at the halt, a sense of balance is more easily recognised. Balance can actually become disturbed by the equipment we use for stability. When we experience nearness to the horse, our legs hang down and we remain deep on its back. When the saddle and stirrups are in place, there is a tendency to push against

them, when the horse's paces become more active. Symptoms of this situation are not being able to keep the foot in the stirrup iron, or not being able to sit down in the saddle.

One pupil who experienced the marked difference between riding her competition pony bareback without the artificiality of a saddle was so reluctant to put it back that she arrived for subsequent lessons without it!

If all saddles fitted both rider and horse, many problems would be resolved at once. Ours is not an ideal world, however, and practicality has to be considered. When the question of good fit arises, the horse should be the main priority. It is imperative that the horse has a well-fitting saddle which sits in balance on its back, well clear of spinal pressure, when the rider is mounted. When a saddle meets

46

Fig 29 Adapting balance using the stirrups.

the demands of balance, the seat of the saddle is in the centre, a point worth checking whenever you ride a strange horse.

Last but not least is the quest for balance in the horse itself, which often has its own problems when asked to carry the weight of a rider. The horse often requires progressive training to recover and develop natural balance when ridden.

The following exercises will help you to develop your awareness of balance, and how it affects you and the horse. There is just one proviso, which is that no horse should be allowed to proceed with a saddle that is pressing down or impinging on the spine in any way when the rider is in the saddle. It is this extra weight, compressing the padding of a worn or ill-fitting saddle, that results in injury, and numnahs only increase the pressure unless the panels are rolled up to increase the padding which is lacking. This is a very temporary expedient to raise the saddle for the duration of the lesson.

Balancing over your own base and the moving base of the horse produces its own challenges, related to the feeling of elevation and to the altered sense of space, to which we all react differently.

To find your balance without trying means being able to let go, firstly of anxieties, and secondly of physical tenseness which so easily comes from a sense of insecurity. It is with these interactions in mind that awareness games have been invented to help you direct your thoughts purposefully and release undue physical strain.

Finding a comfortable way to distribute your body weight will allow you to discover balance for yourself. When the body is out of balance we could hear it

Fig 30   Tape to identify angle of thigh.

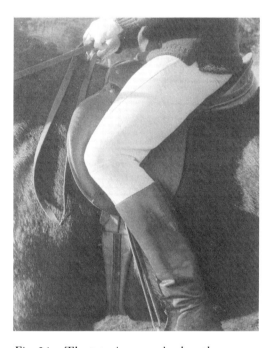

Fig 31   The tape is covered when the rider grips with the knee, causing him to drop the right hand.

complaining if we would only listen.

One pupil's experience explains how these symptoms can be helpful clues in the realignment process. Mary came for lessons with a long-standing apprehension. She was encouraged to see if she could express her apprehension and the reasons for its persistence. The percentage game was used to assess her observations.

'How uptight do you feel out of 100?' she was asked, to which she replied 'About 95 per cent'.

'What does it feel like?' she was then asked. It made her feel sick; her body was responding to the 'sick with fright' feeling. This state of mind clearly interfered with her balance and tightened her seat muscles, thus pitching her forward. This in turn made her feel insecure and even more anxious.

Mary chose to do her awareness exercises in walk, to the extent of spending four lessons doing nothing but noticing one sensation after another as they arose. She began with pain in her lower back. The next twinge was her right hip, then her thigh, knee and left ankle, and finally her toe.

With each twinge she monitored the pain out of ten. This involved her full attention, which increased with each successful experiment. The whole time she was relaxing bit by bit, without realising it. During the fifth lesson she became more active, trotting for a large part of it with enjoyment and a growing feeling of stability. After that her attention was fully diverted to the horse which she went on to school with lively assertiveness, revealing the other side of herself which had been hidden by fear. Once she could let go and sit down in the saddle, which she did by observing and listening to her body, she proved herself to be a perceptive and effective rider.

To sum up:

- There is more to balance than meets the eye.
- You can develop your sense of balance by being aware of the importance of its mental and emotional aspects.
- It is important to experience the feeling of the horse's back without a saddle, if only standing still or walking a few steps with an assistant.
- If a steady horse is available for lunging practice, this would help you to sense the horse's bend on a circle.
- When riding bareback always use a neck strap.
- It is important to appreciate the difference a saddle makes without losing the shadow feeling of the horse's back beneath it.
- Always check that the lowest part of the seat of the saddle is the centre, and that there is room for you to sit comfortably.
- Understand the horse's requirements.
- Recognise that all these things affect the whole – you and your horse – working together.

Helping Hands

Balance is disturbed by being tense. This is often described as 'tied up in knots', both metaphorically and literally, because muscles contract and do not always relax totally. The following awareness games will help to reduce this feeling.

Relaxation is particularly relevant to a rider's hands. Riders can encounter difficulty in this area because good hands depend on balance, which means having sufficient stability to remain in the saddle without using the reins for support. However balanced a rider becomes in the saddle, there is still the horse at the end of the reins. Any inadvertent movement can disturb the horse's mouth and its balance.

Finding the right place to carry the hands is sometimes difficult. The differences of individual proportions need to be taken into consideration. The proportion of the upper part of the body have a bearing on the rider's balance, because when the elbow is set high above the waist, it means the hand will be carried higher than those of a pupil whose elbow hangs below the waist. Obviously the rider who can carry the hand near the withers may well feel more secure. The movement of the elbow joint opening

and closing can be seen when the rider's hands move with the nodding of the horse's head when the horse is walking.

Viewed from the side, the elbow, the hand and the bit in the horse's mouth should be in a straight line. Problems arise when this line is distorted.

BALL GAME 1

The following awareness game will help riders to recognise where their hands feel natural. The game requires a soft foam sponge ball about the size of a golf ball, which can be bought at a pet shop or cut off a sponge. Ride with the ball in one hand and then change it to the other. See which hand you prefer, and whether it is

Fig 32 Notice how the relationship of the rider's elbow and waist influences the angle of the forearm.

Fig 33 Compare this with Fig 32.

Fig 34   *The rein line should run directly from the horse's mouth to the rider's elbow.*

Fig 35   *Hand position and rein line incorrect.*

the inside or outside hand when going round to the left. Repeat the exercise going the other way round to see if it makes any difference. Ask yourself the following questions:

1. Is there any difference on the left rein when you change the ball from one hand to the other?
2. Do you prefer it in your outside or inside hand?
3. What difference do you notice between your left and right hand?
4. Does it make any difference if you reverse the process on the other rein?
5. What happens when you change the ball from one hand to the other?

You may not have time to notice the actual change-over. Once you have come to some conclusions about your right and left hands, give your attention to the change-over itself. Notice how you do the change-over, where your hands go in space and, if possible, what the horse does.

Your answers to the first two questions will reveal how you use your hands naturally, and what level and distance from your body is right for you. The third one may still remain unanswered if your full attention has been involved with your hands. This can be your final assessment in relation to possible changes in your horse, and how you respond to one another. The horse often responds to the first change of hands by lowering and relaxing its head and neck, which will make a marked change in its balance and your comfort.

Fig 36   This rider is tense when the ball is in the right hand.

Fig 37   He is more relaxed when he is about to change it over. Notice how the horse responds.

BALL GAME 2

For this game you will need two balls. You can use either two soft golf balls, two soft yellow tennis balls or two pieces of foam sponge cut to size. Hold one in each hand, with each just visible between your thumb and first finger. Keep your hands on the 'rein line'.

Now ride about and see which sensations the balls magnify. Observe your hands to see whether you lose sight of the balls between the thumb and first finger, and note any unusual feelings as you change pace, change direction, slow down or halt. Pay attention to each movement at a time and go along with what is happening to you and your horse.

You may discover that you squash the ball in the right hand more than the left one, or that the feeling of the rein may be softer as the horse responds to your sensitivity. What each individual discovers, or their way of interpreting it, cannot be predicted.

This ball game was being watched by a retired police inspector from the mounted section. He was so impressed with the results that he was going to pass on the idea for the use of recruits in training. As with all games, however, there are those who do not like playing them. If the balls are rejected as being a distraction, this must be accepted as the pupil's prerogative. Yet most pupils find them informative and relaxing, and know just the right moment to dispense with their use.

Like the shadow imprint of the horse's back beneath the saddle, the ball leaves a shadow imprint in the hand. Riders do not become addicted to or dependent on these teaching aids. They may become mental sets, rituals which competitors can use to boost positive thinking. Perhaps

53

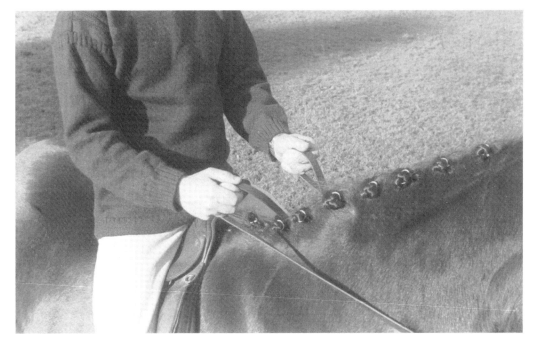

Fig 38   The rider holds a foam ball in each hand.

this is where certain sporting superstitions have their origins. John Currie, the skater, is said to put his right sock and right boot on before a competition. He says that this puts him in the right psychological frame of mind.

The use of the ball magnifies subtle sensations which, once felt, continue to be remembered. It is often difficult to recognise specific sensations when they are first encountered, but when they are enlarged it makes them more clear. The use of the exercise lies in the interest it creates, the awareness it develops and the relaxation which is the outcome. Once the sequence works for pupils, they often carry a spare ball and push it inside their glove to induce calmness when under stress. There will be an automatic response because the rider trusts the process.

In time he or she dispenses with the actual balls and visualises them instead. A spin-off from this routine is the developing harmony between the horse's mouth and the rider's hand, which is such a vital line of communication.

Taping the Trot

RISING TROT

The trot is a pace of two-time in which the horse moves diagonal pairs of legs alternately, and to which the rider can sit or rise. When pupils start riding the priority is, more often than not, learning to rise at the trot before the rider has had time to establish any sense of balance.

The rising trot requires balance, co-ordination and a sense of rhythm to be smooth and effortless, so it is understandably difficult for novice riders to produce a synchronised movement. The exaggerated effort involved can leave a legacy of imbalance which is still evident at more advanced levels.

The reasons why this situation arises is, first, that it can be more comfortable than a sitting trot on some horses and, secondly, because the horse's back will suffer less. A third reason is the lack of time in which to develop a comfortable sitting trot, from which the rising trot would emerge more easily. On the Continent, pupils spend longer on the lunge learning to sit deeply in the saddle.

If riders learnt to do sitting trot in balance, there would be fewer rising trot problems. It does not follow that going up and down to rise, as you may have been taught, means that you can sit to the trot as a result. If you are out of balance in one situation, you will almost certainly be out of balance in the other.

The rising trot is used for young horses whose physique is still maturing. It is also used in early riding lessons as a short cut to stability when riding out. Riders 'post' for the comfort of the horse and themselves, which leads to the question of diagonals, in which the horse moves its legs in trot and in which one or other pair of legs will receive all of the rider's weight. This will happen constantly unless the rider knows how to change over to the other diagonal.

Rising trot is used much of the time at the novice riding level and when schooling young horses to allow their developing muscles more freedom. It is also a practical way to ride out in the country, when both horse and rider benefit from the intermittent movement. Sitting in the saddle for long periods would reduce the circulation in the horse's back and in the rider's seat, exposing both to soreness.

Two questions arise when you rise to the trot. One is 'Are you in balance?' and the second is 'Do you recognise which of the diagonals you are sitting on when you are going up and down in rising trot?' Recognising the diagonal steps of the horse is not nearly as simple as is sometimes implied. If a rider felt less guilty about not seeing what happens, many more might admit to this hidden difficulty, which can continue for years. An instructor once disclosed his problem after he was qualified. We should not therefore be surprised if fear of seeming stupid prevents pupils asking for help, for too little time is given to this body/eye synchronisation and too many riders are left uncertain about their ability to ride on both diagonals.

To be able to change diagonals prevents not only fatigue in the horse, but lopsided muscular development and strain. Therefore, it is important to know which diagonal you use, which is your favourite or natural one, and how to change from one to the other so that you use the horse evenly.

Here is an exercise to help the recognition of diagonal movement in the horse's trot. You will need coloured insulating tape cut in strips to put along the line of the horse's shoulder (see Figs 39 to 41). If you wish, you can use a contrasting colour on the opposite shoulder. When you have done this, work in trot, watching them move backwards and forwards until your eye has time to pick up what is happening to the horse's shoulders. Do not expect to get your eye in at once. Ball

Fig 39 Riding on the left diagonal, rising as the near shoulder comes forward.

Fig 40 Sitting as it comes back.

Fig 41   Riding on the right diagonal, rising as the off shoulder
goes forward.

Fig 42   Sitting as the off shoulder comes back.

game players need time to do this, and it is the same for you as a rider. Gradually feel your body moving up as one tape goes forward, and sitting as it comes back. This is the diagonal on which you are said to be riding. To change it, miss out a rise, when you will feel a double sit. Now sit and set off on the new diagonal. Keep practising until it becomes second nature. When riding in the arena it helps the horse's balance if you ride on the outside diagonal, rising as the outside shoulder goes forward and sitting as it comes back. This also means both diagonals are used as the changes of rein (the direction in which you travel round the arena) are made.

This detailed explanation has been included because of the number of pupils who encounter the problem and hesitate to admit it. It thus remains unresolved for too long. We lose our eye without constant practice. Even when diagonals are more easily recognised, our eye can lose its ability to focus, so do give yourself time to get your eye in if you are not riding regularly.

The tape can be useful in canter strike-off when leading legs may be difficult to recognise, but it should not be continued so long that looking down becomes a habit.

Pupils often need to be assisted with another aspect of the rising trot, one which can easily arise when balance is lacking. This particular difficulty arises when the rider is still perched on top of the horse, is riding too short and is left behind the movement. The rise then looks awkward, which it can do even at exam and competition level.

Whatever the root cause, the outcome is a laborious heave too far out of the saddle and a loss of balance returning to it. The time lapse taken for these two movements is longer than the diagonal beat of the horse's feet, so the rider bobs along quite unaware that he or she is not in time with the horse. The main aim would appear to be to get up and let the down take care of itself. One of the most difficult corrections to make is in the rising trot. Few of us get up from or sit down in chairs without misusing our bodies, and what we do off the horse we magnify when we are on it.

Before checking the rider's awareness, a basic balance check needs to be done. If the stirrups are too short, the rider needs to make some readjustments. Short stirrup leathers tend to indicate tension somewhere, preventing the letting go which allows the rider to sit deeper in the saddle. Once the pupil feels more comfortable, he or she can be asked to observe the beat of the horse's shoulder movement, marked with tape for clarity, and to count it out aloud. Having done that, the pupil counts the beat of the rising trot movement, and is asked to check whether it is identical to the shoulder's. Pupils seem to notice quite easily when they are behind the beat and this alone produces a natural synchronisation.

So far so good in relation to awareness, but to develop synchronisation without instructions means giving pupils an exercise which holds their attention, creates awareness and lets them relax into the desired result. The most useful exercise is to ask them to keep up the counting while alternately using rising and sitting trot, for whatever number of steps feels comfortable.

Another option is to forget the up part of the rising trot and concentrate on the 'bounce'. Some pupils have used 'bounce sit' as their way of thinking themselves into a smooth rising trot. Just as pupils recognise being off-beat once their awareness is drawn to it, they quickly recognise when they are on time.

SITTING TROT

This discussion on the trot leaves us with the sitting trot, which often tends to get left to the last. But it has every right to be the main priority if a really well-balanced position is to develop from the start.

When the time does come to practise it, pupils can be exposed to some pretty tough treatment, trotting round on uncomfortable horses without stirrups in the hope it will 'jelly' them down in the saddle, if only from sheer fatigue. Riding without stirrups is a waste of time and effort if riders raise their knees to recover their stirrup irons when the exercise is over. Unless the mirror image of length and depth is kept, there is no point to this activity. How the stirrup irons are replaced is vital to the end result, and depends on how much – if at all – the pupils have relaxed without their stirrups, and how much of the extension of the legs can be accommodated once the foot is in the stirrup iron. The knee should hardly move at all when doing this. Asking pupils to keep the feeling of depth when they retake their stirrups often means they need to lengthen the stirrup leather.

Working without stirrups is regarded as a sure way of getting riders down in the saddle, but it can be an agonising process, in which case tension will prevent the object of the exercise taking place.

It seems there has to be a compromise when schooled horses for trainee riders are not always available, and this compromise must come from the horses that are available. Horses jog quite happily out hacking or on the way to a meet, so it does them no harm to jog for riders who want to feel more comfortable. This can prove to be a very useful exercise and works the horse more than might be thought. The rider is told to jog as slowly as he or she wishes providing the horse keeps going. What happens is that the horse has to use its hind legs in order not to lapse into walk, and the rider feels relaxed. Before long, by mutual consent, a more forward trot emerges, with the horse and rider moving in mutual comfort and accord. If at this point the rider is asked to rise without losing the feeling of closeness, he or she will move smoothly and unobtrusively into a smooth easy trot, totally in balance with the horse. In a safe situation, sitting trot can be done bareback, which allows the rider to feel the muscles of the horse as it moves.

On one occasion when a pupil was working on sitting trot, she was asked to describe in two words what the feeling was. Her reply was 'buoyant and swinging'. After that, those words evoked that feeling for her whenever she wanted it.

The Word Game

Words often have more impact than we realise. When pupils are asked to describe sensations they have to use words to express themselves, and these words can become tools for them to use. The coach's choice of word often detracts from this effect; it must be the learner who describes what is being felt.

Here is a story which shows the magic of word power. Frances, an experienced pupil, had always longed to look elegant. However hard she tried, this feeling eluded her, until one day she was asked to think of a rider she admired and to picture them in detail. She was then asked to role play what she thought they did. When she was absorbed in this experiment, she began to look dramatically different. On returning to the coach she said: 'I feel so inflated; it's terrific. I do feel elegant, and the feeling comes from my diaphragm. What's more, I am breathing more deeply.' She never lost her poise after this breakthrough.

The Canter in Natural Riding

Pupils have revealed numerous worries about this pace, which will be discussed in Chapter 6. In view of these barriers, more explicit information is required to reduce such worries and put the canter in proper perspective, so that it can be enjoyed. At this stage, it is enough to remember that horses can also find it difficult unless they are naturally well balanced, so riders need to be patient with themselves and their horses, to keep calm and hold their attention on one difficulty at a time. Forcing the pace through anxiety results in resistance in both rider and horse.

The following dismounted exercise will help the feeling of balance on your own feet and your awareness of weight distribution.

1. Stand evenly on both feet, noticing where you feel the most weight. Are you in fact carrying it evenly on both feet?
2. Now bend your knees slightly as you would in the saddle, noticing how the weight changes. Where is it now?
3. Relax and stand upright.
4. Repeat the exercise, but push your knees out as you bend them, checking the change of feeling in your feet and knees. Where is the weight now?
5. Relax and stand upright.
6. Repeat the knee bending, but this time put your heels down hard against the floor, noticing the effect on your balance. What happened?
7. Remember how it felt when you pushed your weight down on to your heels, and the effect it had on your balance. In this position your weight would be thrown back. If you relate this imbalance to your position in the saddle, you will realise that pushing your heels down will result in being behind the horse's movement.

Repeat these exercises from time to time because they create awareness of the subtle changes which take place as we alter the position of our bodies, and are particularly relevant in rising trot.

4 The Horse

In this chapter the spotlight of our attention is focused on the horse, this unique species which contributes so valuably to our human experience. By recognising the extraordinary process through which the horse has travelled on the long journey of evolution, we can appreciate more fully the remarkable adaptations which have taken place in order to guarantee its survival.

Forty to fifty million years ago, a small three-toed animal browsed in the primeval undergrowth, providing a tasty meal for marauding predators. The horse we know today bears little resemblance to this lowly ancestor, except for the two rudimentary toes which now form the splint bones on either side of the cannon bone of all four legs.

Much later, the domestication of the horse in its more evolved form increased the range of human freedom while depriving the horse of its liberty. What both shared, however, was greater protection from natural predators.

The early predators of both human and horse have been superseded by contemporary ones. In our case, they are the pressures of modern life; for the horse, the indirect effects of these pressures, together with the additional hardship for a herd-orientated animal of living an unnaturally isolated life.

The basic instincts of flight and fight are still innate in humans and in horses, and they surface in different forms. The fact that conditioning may have supressed their expression does not mean that these instincts do not exist. It is this repression which results in the residual muscle tension we have already discussed, and which so often comes between us and our mount.

For centuries the horse has carried history on its back, not only as the main form of transportation but also as a worker and tiller of the land, until its enduring usefulness to civilisation diminished in the face of mechanisation.

The reversal of the horse's decline has largely been due to the indelible fascination which it has always held for its admirers, and the changing economic climate which has opened up opportunities for many more people to ride. The tide has now turned in the horse's favour. For some the horse has become a status symbol, often at the mercy of inexperienced owners, while for others it has opened up new vistas of leisure hours spent in happy companionship.

The horse's future now looks well established and, in exchange for its contribution to our lives, we should reciprocate by taking responsibility for its welfare. This concern includes the minimising, through good management, of discomforts, ill health and unsoundness. Good management requires observation, knowledge, understanding and communication. It is a vital part of good riding, for there is no pleasure in working an unfit or unhappy horse. Riding can have repercussions on management too, for a horse who is fretful in its work does not thrive as well as a contented one.

To respect the rights of an animal which cannot speak for itself, we need to

Fig 43   Lunging: view of the horse from the front.

Fig 44   Lunging: view of the horse from the side.

Fig 45   Lunging: view of the horse from the rear. Notice the
tapes on its quarters to show its movement.

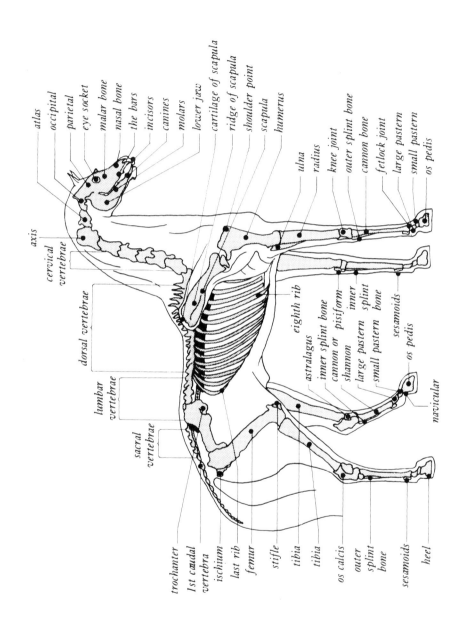

Fig 46   The framework of the horse.

64

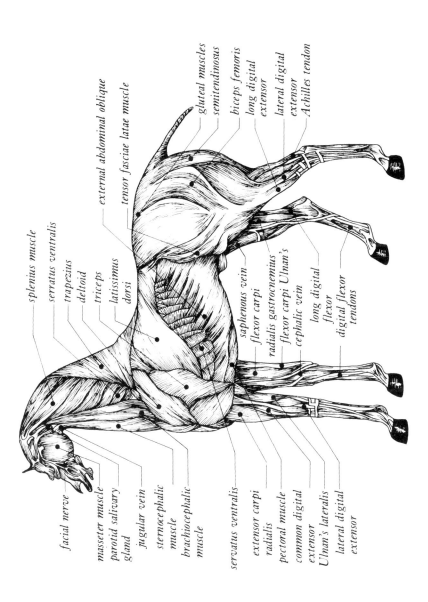

Fig 47 The musculature of the horse.

develop eyes which see, ears which hear, a sense of touch which feels and, most of all, our intuition. When the horse feels safe in your hands, it will pay you the supreme compliment of trust which more than makes up for the loss, which we take for granted, of its natural liberty.

Looking at the Horse

In wishing to know their horses better, riders often complain they do not always have the opportunity to watch their own horses being ridden. The following project is used to develop the power of observation, and has proved effective in helping riders to see more precisely the shape and movement of the animal on which they sit, sometimes so precariously.

These dismounted exercises allow the rider to pay full attention to their horse's mode of locomotion. The use of a lunge rein is helpful, or alternatively an assistant can lead a horse up and down in walk and in trot. The primary aim of the spectator is to study the whole body of the horse from head to tail, watching the movement of the muscles, joints, ears and nostrils, eyes and feet. The horse must be viewed from the side, from the front and then the rear as it goes away from you. Study the horse from all possible angles, noticing the bend of the joints, the movement of the quarters, the swing of the rib-cage and the interplay of muscles.

If a few interested friends are available you can turn this into a movement spotting game, in which everyone lets their eyes travel over the horse, asking themselves what they notice the most. Is it the bend of the knee, the stifle, or even the hip joint which I have not noticed in such

detail before? This is a particularly interesting and informative method of learning the points of the horse and its anatomy.

When you have identified specific areas of interest, stop the horse and mark the spot with a piece of insulating tape or a self-adhesive label. Repeat this process over and over again for ten minutes. You will be surprised at the areas of mobility which catch your eye – the muscles of the quarters, the shoulders, the back and neck. Each time you label an area, feel it with your hands and, if the horse is quiet, pick up the leg and gently flex the joints you have noticed. This handling of the horse imprints the information more firmly on your unconscious. You become more and more familiar with the structure and shape and movement of your horse's body, and you will gain a much deeper appreciation than just getting up and sitting on its back.

Many pupils have been surprised at the movement in the area of the withers, impressing it upon their awareness by walking beside the horse with their hands on this point of its body. This movement can also be felt in front of the saddle when you are mounted. The continuous swing and sway of the whole body in locomotion is not always felt or understood by the rider. This binocular view of the horse makes it easier for the rider to appreciate how it moves when at liberty, and how when we are in the saddle we can impede this natural movement and balance.

However many times this game is played with a group of riders, the horse ends up covered with stickers, and someone always finds a new area of interest. If the horse has twenty-two muscles in its neck and sixteen in its ears, this discovery is not surprising. The objective behind the exercise is to develop the rider's eye, which becomes sharper with practice; to develop the sense of feel for shape, texture and temperature of the horse's body; and generally to become more closely acquainted with the horse. The result of a half-hour session spent in this way can be remarkably constructive.

Communication

Communication is a means of exchanging messages, whether with a person or with an animal, and it is the lucidity with which we do this that enables them to be understood clearly. We can easily fail the horse by not always understanding the problem it has in recognising our directions. Interpersonal relationships can be upset in just the same way, by taking it for granted that another person understands us, when in fact they do not.

Unrealistic expectations often cloud the real issue so we have problems putting ourselves in someone else's shoes, at the same time expecting them to be able to put on our own. The horse is a foreigner in a strange land, and developing the imagination to 'put on the horse's shoes', feeling the desperation of being unable to understand what is being asked, would make for more sympathetic riders. Nothing is more frustrating to good communication than crossed wires.

On what then do we base our hope that we can develop a dialogue with our horse so that its education can proceed smoothly to the point where it is able to understand the commands we give it? The answer is to make sure that it is a dialogue and not a boring, nagging monologue. This means listening and responding to the horse

when the horse responds to you. The conversation needs to be clear and logical. The rider must give a clear signal and continue it until there is a response. When the horse reponds, the respite from the signal acts as a reward, and can be underlined with verbal praise or patting. To put it briefly, the sequence is request, response, reward. If trainers and riders kept meticulously to this basic formula both misunderstanding and resistance would be reduced. Instead, however, human over-eagerness tries to maintain a response by continuing the request after it has been heeded, which to the horse then becomes a punishment.

A typical example of this is the horse with a lazy walk being kicked numb by the rider. Over and over again the horse, moving forward to the rider's leg, is kicked on to keep it going. The horse soon realises in self-defence that if it walks on there is no reward. What is the point of bothering to respond in the first place?

I once had an interesting experience when I was asked to improve the obedience of a very sluggish four-year-old mare which had become impervious to the whip and the spur. The first request given by the rider's legs produced no response from the horse, so the mark out of ten was zero. The same signal was repeated several times, with the same result. By now the audience and I were laughing. The horse was asked once more, and this time the muscles contracted as if it was going to step forward. This earned half a mark. The next attempt produced a step and the mark went up to one, while the rider remained relaxed and aware without increasing the strength of the signal. A few more repetitions produced an improving scale of marks up to five. The horse began to walk forward, at which point the exercise was terminated. What had happened? I asked the audience if they had heard the horse's deep sigh of relief. It had been holding its breath in defence against an erroneous communication. From that point onward the horse improved and in due course became a successful all-round competitor.

I have used the same tactics with other benumbed and bewildered mounts whose riders have forgotten to make time to say thank you for small responses. Learning takes place slowly, and learning a new language means remembering a few words and repeating them until they become familiar. The horse's vocabulary starts with a simple A, B, C. As the late Captain Edy Goldman said, 'It moves from simplicity to complexity and back to simplicity. When this happens, thought alone seems to be the only message needed between rider and horse.'

'Talking' to the horse involves all of our senses, which are continually receiving and sending out information. *Body language* speaks more clearly than words, and it is this subconscious signalling system which sometimes contradicts verbal directions and intended specific ones. Mannerisms and emotions make undercover statements which register with the horse.

Verbal communication can still often express our innermost feeling. The voice with its wide range of tone can be a powerful tool in calming, stimulating and controlling the horse. It can also be a frightening weapon if uncontrolled emotion takes over and tempers are lost.

The *tactile sense* can sometimes pick up what the eye can miss. When a horse is lame, for example, the eye cannot see heat in the leg until it produces swelling. It is

touch which transmits the messages to the horse when mounted – the touch on the reins with the hands, the feel of the rider's seat in the saddle, the rider's legs touching the horse's side.

Sight provides so much of our information in everyday life that it is difficult to imagine the life of a blind person who has to develop the tactile and auditory senses to compensate. The horse's field of vision is different from the human one, and understanding how the horse uses its eyes makes some of its reactions more predictable. Try putting the width of your hand on the bridge of your nose as if it was the horse's wide forehead. Though you need to take into account the fact that your peripheral vision is limited compared with the horse's, with its eye set as it is more to the side, it will give you some idea of how the horse views its world.

It may also help to demonstrate the horse's difficulty in focusing on objects directly in front and behind without turning its head, and explains why some horses have shying and jumping problems. A horse also cannot see what is below eye level four feet in front of it, and this may account for horses jumping too high over low fences, though they do often develop a jumping memory to help them assess the correct take-off zone.

To sit on a horse and expect it to see what we see is a false premise. It leads to unrealistic expectations, and riders often blame the horse for what is in fact their own lack of insight.

I was once at a pony club camp where a small cross-country course had been built for the novice riders. It proved to be a great success, apart from one particular fence which every horse refused. I decided to test the course myself, so I mounted and rode round the course, fence by fence, until I arrived at the one in question. It produced the same result as before. None of the ponies would jump the small wall on to a sandy path. I felt that this was so unusual that I dismounted and viewed the fence from horse's eye level. On the far side there was a bank, which, because of an optical illusion, appeared to slope down behind the wall. On seeing this, the horses were faced with the solidity of the barrier, with no ground visible on which to land the other side. This experience taught me the value of investigating thoroughly the horse's point of view, from all angles.

Fit to Work

We owe it to the horse to know when it is in a suitable state of health to work. A horse is said to be fit when it can perform its allotted task without loss of condition. The degree of muscle tone needed will vary with different demands, ranging from weekend riding to hunting, racing, show-jumping, eventing and long distance riding. Each activity needs a carefully planned regime to ensure that the horse has the long-term stamina required for the hunting season, or the quick burst of speed on a particular racing day.

Nowadays, it is almost a science to bring the horse to peak condition at the right time. The competitive world has raised the demands made on equine stamina just as much as it has raised the level of human potential. Consequently, developing the exact level of fitness has become an art in itself. Even the less exotic levels of riding, where enjoyment and relaxation are the main motivation, still require a certain fitness for the horse to do its work easily. After all, a horse which has spent a lazy week in a good pasture will not be ready for a sudden burst of activity at the weekend – such an expectation is tantamount to jogging immediately after the Sunday lunch. This sort of treatment of the horse's body is going to put unnecessary strain on vital organs and indirectly on the limbs, and is therefore counter-productive.

Situations often arise where owners take their horses on courses of instruction, where they work longer hours than they do at home, perhaps for two or three consecutive days. Even a fit horse can feel the effects of this stepped-up exercise routine, and can pull out of the stable very stiff and sore at some point in the programme. This is not always seen for what it is, and the horse may be blamed for resistance.

A classic example of this situation was when a school horse was used on a dressage course. After two days of improving its balance, it suddenly reverted to being so much on the forehand that the rider felt out of control and was greatly disappointed. On investigation, the musculature of the horse's back and quarters was found to be very tender.

The same reaction can occur in the horse's neck when working too intensively on one direction in order to overcome a problem. It is therefore well worthwhile checking the horse's body while grooming to see just how any change in exercise has had physical repercussions.

It is not only physical changes which warrant our attention. Mental changes can also have an impact. Any schooling for the horse is like putting a child in a classroom, where peak levels of concentration may not last more than ten minutes at a time. It stands to reason that a horse which is schooled intensively for forty minutes is being expected to do more than most human beings are capable of. Riders often complain that their horses are inconsistent, or that they do not keep their heads still, without considering the state of the horse's muscles and mind. It has been discovered that children's study is more successful when they are given frequent rests, and this applies even more when working with an animal.

Without meaning to, we can overload our horses with unnecessary pressures, ignoring the signs of stress in their bodies and general demeanour, signs which an aware rider learns to recognise. When something is amiss we must always ask where and when it hurts. The horse cannot explain but, as riders, we can learn to decipher the horse's message. Perceptive people feel at once that something is not quite right, often without knowing exactly why, and will therefore nip problems in the bud. Good management is the foundation of enjoyable riding with a happy horse and it pays enormous dividends to increase your powers of observation and sensitivity.

Training

When a horse starts its education, the question of fitness is related to growth rather than to endurance. The young horse needs to be maintained in good condition, enabling it to mature and to provide energy for its work. A knowledgeable trainer will make sure that an unsuitable regime does not result in volatile behaviour, the objective being gentle, appropriate, progressive exercises.

Not all horses, however, have the benefit of systematic and logical training, and there are times without number when semi-broken horses end up in novice hands, a situation which creates frustrating and sometimes frightening problems for both horse and rider.

With experienced help, and the owner's patience and perseverance, the problem may be solved and a surprisingly happy partnership may develop. Any semi-schooled horse arriving in a new home is likely to suffer from confusion and insecurity until some understanding can be reached and its physical condition monitored. The horse's metabolism is affected by its environment as a whole, of which its education is an important part.

Unconducive conditions cause stress which, if not resolved, eventually detract from the horse's well-being. The horse will be more vulnerable to injury and disease, and less willing to learn.

Ideally, the horse should grow up in a healthy environment until it is considered sufficiently mature to begin its education, at about three or four years old. This should proceed calmly and progressively on the lunge, where it learns simple words of command and finds its balance by circling in both directions. As the horse is able to extend its activities through increasing its muscle development, so its food intake should be adjusted to supply the needs both of growth and of increasing exercise.

Once the riding stage is reached, when the giving of commands is handed over from trainer to the rider, more work will be involved to help the horse to recover its natural balance. This is done through simple school movements; what might be called gentle gymnastic exercises. The four basic principles to be established in a horse's training are as follows:

• The horse should be calm.
• It should go forward freely.
• It should be straight, its hind legs following the path of its forelegs on whatever line it is travelling.
• It should develop a regular footfall in its paces, the speed of the beat being called the 'tempo'.

Obviously all these attributes are not asked for at once. Forward movement and calmness are the priorities, and the other principles gradually emerge as the horse's balance develops.

One advantage which the aware rider brings to this situation and, in fact, all through the horse's training, is the ability to ask just for one thing at a time. If you say to your young horse, 'That was a good halt, but you have lifted your head', and you immediately correct this second factor, the reward for stopping gets lost, becoming a reprimand rather than a reward.

This is a common occurrence, leading to resistance and to conflict. When the rider pays attention to an initial gesture and rewards it at once, the horse not only relaxes but begins to understand. If you have a whole list of things which could have been better, you will end up confusing the horse. The horse must often ask itself what we are on about with our constant demands about what it should do and where it should place itself from step to step. If our questions are continual what the horse gives us will decrease. Reverse this and you will find, as a pupil of mine did recently, that 'the less I ask, the more I get'. Keep this paradox in mind. We are not always logical in our requests to the horse.

Considerable patience is required by the trainer, for the horse needs time to develop both physically and mentally. Horses who live in happy and healthy conditions will go on maturing and improving well into their late teens. This seems to prove that horses, like people, are more content when they are involved in interesting work and happy companionship.

Saddlery

This outline of the horse's education brings the important question of saddlery to the fore. It is an important topic because the horse's comfort and efficiency depend upon it. It is important that both rider and horse feel comfortable

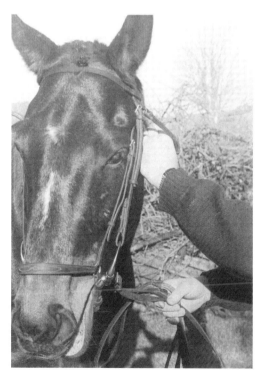

Fig 48   Measuring the throat lash.

and in control. Not least among reasons why the correct choice of saddlery is important is that its price now makes any mistakes very expensive ones.

So what are the priorities? Obviously, a suitable saddle and bridle are the main items that spring to mind, with perhaps a numnah and, if the horse is stabled, adequate rugs for its comfort. If the horse is going to compete or travel, boots and bandages will form part of its equipment. Once you start thinking about competitions, your horse's wardrobe can be more extensive – and, of course, more expensive.

The following suggestions are not intended to be a treatise on saddlery, rather a guide to common mistakes which are often made in the way it is fitted, mistakes which are detrimental to both horse and, in due course, the rider. We have already looked closely at the horse, and now it is equally important to examine what the horse is to wear when we ride it.

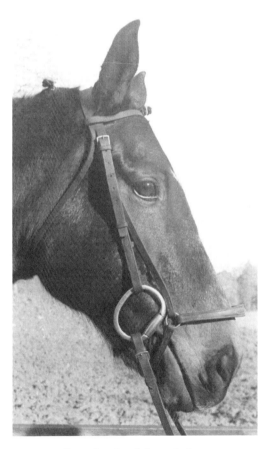

Fig 49   Brow band and throat lash are too tight and drop noseband too big.

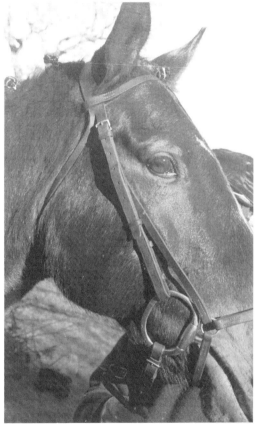

Fig 50   How this cuts into the gullet.

BRIDLES

If we begin with the simple snaffle bridle, the points to check are the brow band, the throat lash and the noseband. If the brow band is too small it puts the headpiece of the bridle forward out of line and presses on the base of the ears. The throat lash must not interfere with the gullet when the horse flexes at the poll. You may be able to push your fist through to measure it and yet it still looks tight, but did you notice how you nearly guillotined the

Fig 51   Correctly fitted bridle.

horse on the far side when you tested it in this way? Your eye is often a better guide. If you look at the throat lash lying roughly half-way down the cheekbone, you will be nearer the mark. Flex the horse at the poll to check there is ample room. Horses who have their gullet and windpipe restricted will not want to accept the bit or go very far.

When it comes to nosebands, the drop noseband can cause the horse pain if it is done up like a girth, as it so often is. It restricts the circulation and presses on the sharp bone at the back of the horse's jaw. It does serve a purpose, but it can be abused. If your horse resents having it done up, you will know why. Try putting your finger between the jaw-bone and the noseband. Find out if your horse really needs one all the time. Monitor this piece of equipment carefully and ask what purpose it serves for your horse. Make sure it is fitted above the nostrils on the nasal bone and not, as one pupil thought, pulled tight over the nose to stop the horse breathing in order to give more control.

The fitting of a jointed snaffle is sometimes easier said than done, because horses have smaller mouths than people imagine. As a result, bits are often too wide and have to be raised excessively to stop them banging on the horse's teeth. The result of this is an exaggerated nutcracker action which presses on the horse's molars. This distorts the true action of the snaffle which, when it is the right size and correctly adjusted, fits snugly and firmly up into the corner of the mouth. When bits are raised too high in the mouth, they cause considerable pressure on the poll, making it almost impossible to insert a finger in the head-piece of the bridle. Another useful check

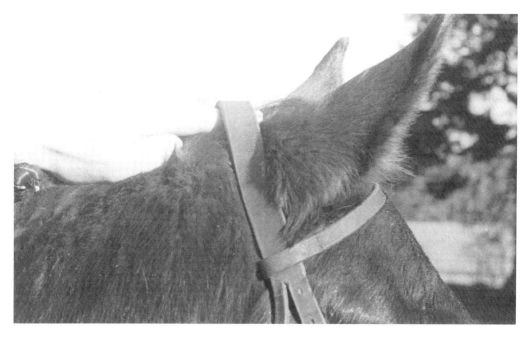

Fig 52   Testing for poll pressure.

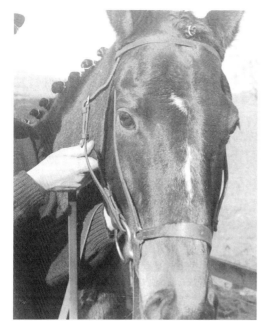

Fig 53   Checking for slackness in the
cheek piece when contact is taken up in
the bit.

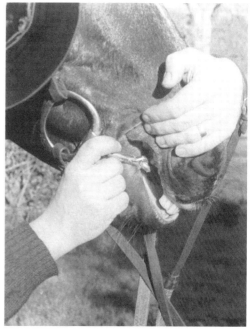

Fig 54   Checking to see if the bit is
hanging too low in the horse's mouth.

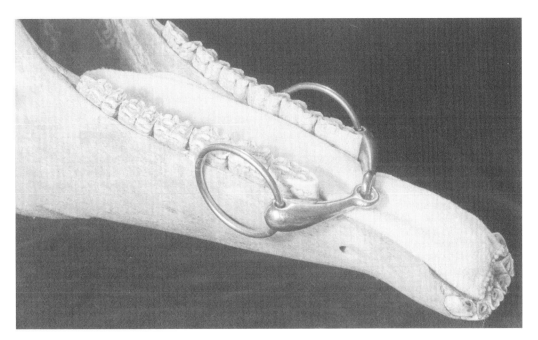

Fig 55   The bit is too big and pinching molars.

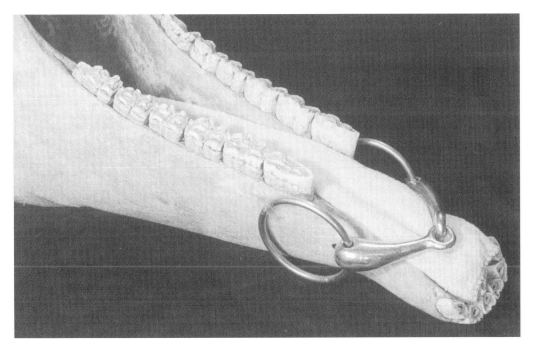

*Fig 56   The bit is too low and would catch the tushes of a
gelding.*

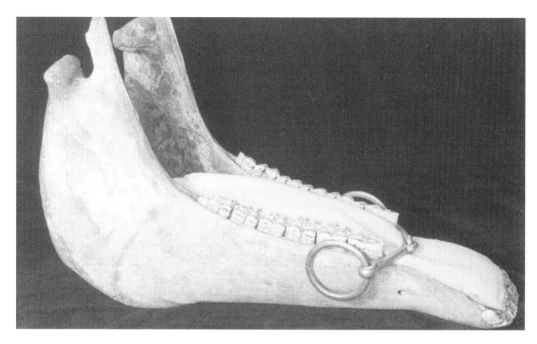

Fig 57   *Correct fitting with less pinching action.*

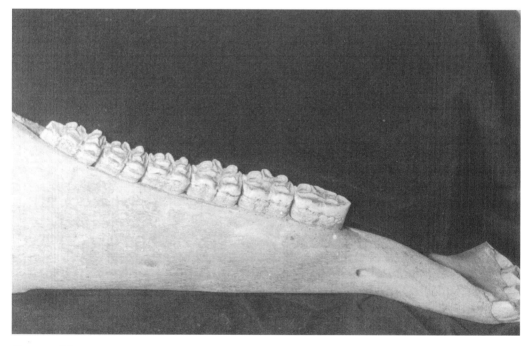

Fig 58   *Notice the sharp edge of the molars in a five-year-old mare.*

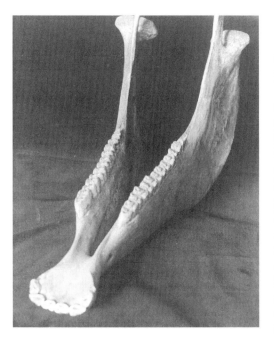

Fig 59   Showing the narrow gap between the upper and lower teeth of a Clydesdale mare.

is to take up a contact in the reins, noticing if the cheek piece of the bridle becomes slack. If it does, then the bit is too low and will ride up and down in the mouth when the contact on the reins varies.

When fitting a bridle, do be aware of your horse's teeth, for no amount of juggling with different bits will solve anything if the horse's molars have become sharp. Once the teeth have been rasped it is not only the bit that will feel more comfortable, but the horse will also be able to chew its food more efficiently. Figs 55 to 59 show how the fitting and size of the bit relate to the bones of the horse's jaw and its teeth.

SADDLES

The saddle will be the biggest outlay. It must fit both the rider and the horse, and can be designed for general use or for a particular use, if you specialise. The saddle should not press on the horse's spine nor pinch the sides of the spine. This must be tested when the rider is in the saddle. You should leave a space beneath the pommel in which two fingers can be inserted. The saddle must be balanced, meaning that the lowest part should be the centre. The saddle should have some leeway in its length for the rider's seat. If the saddle is too small the rider will be sitting over the thick padding under the cantle and not in the lowest part in the middle, making it impossible for him or her to be in balance (*See* Figs 60 and 61 for correct and incorrect fittings).

Saddle problems often arise during courses, when pupils attend with their own horses and unsuitable saddles. It is surprising how many are used which do not fit the horse or the rider. The only instant recourse to help the horse is to roll up the flaps of a numnah to supplement the deficient stuffing in the saddle. This usually lifts the saddle clear of the spine as a temporary measure, and avoids the disappointment of a pupil having to withdraw from a lesson. There is really no excuse for a horse having to work in an ill-fitting saddle, which can cause discomfort and possibly injury. Saddles need restuffing and restitching from time to time, and regular overhaul is as important for a saddle as for a car.

Boots and bandages need careful application, because the tension that can be exerted can restrict the blood supply. It is possible for horses to go lame simply because of wrongly applied bandages. A good way to practise is on your own arm or leg, when you will appreciate the

Fig 60   *A well-fitting general-purpose saddle, clearing the withers.*

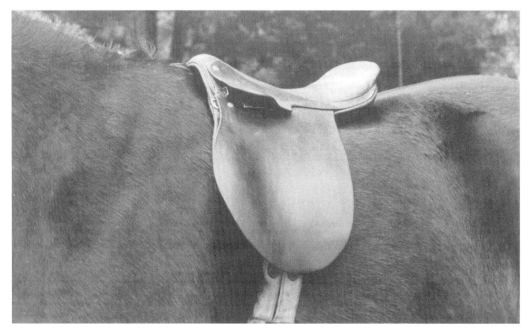

Fig 61   *This saddle is an old-fashioned hunting saddle – it is too low over the withers and has a very flat seat.*

difference between support, protection, and suppression of the circulation.

Soundness

The horse needs to be well and happy to work with zest and should be sound in wind, limb, eye, heart and back. The horse's back is stressed in this book because of its vulnerability and, to some extent, the invisibility of any unsoundness. Lameness of limbs is usually more obvious than the degree of discomfort a horse suffers in its back.

There are many horses working with chronically tender backs, a problem of which their riders appear to be unaware. Though the symptoms are evident, they are not recognised for what they are. They get lost in the round of everyday incidents, and are reflected in comments such as 'My horse won't stand still to be mounted' or 'He always drops his back when I get on'. The slight stiffness in the hind legs when moving forward or in upward transitions might be indicative of discomfort, but it too passes unobserved by the rider.

If you inspect such a horse's back carefully, it will be quite tender when the muscles on either side are pressed. Sometimes the spine itself is sore and may well indicate the need not only for rest, but also for a visit from the vet. Acute cases will nearly collapse when the back is tested, but usually by this time the horse's performance has deteriorated enough to draw attention to the fact that something is sadly amiss.

The horse's back, which looks so strong and substantial, was not designed by nature to carry a rider, or any other weight for that matter. The saddle itself

Fig 62 Inspecting the horse's back.

adds more than six kilograms (thirteen pounds) to the load, and in its rigidity can become an unrelenting medium between the horse's back and the rider. If the horse is in poor condition, the comfortable fitting of a saddle may be almost impossible. Horses' backs are particularly exposed to accidents while falling, and to strain while slipping, jumping and mounting. Horses which are overworked when young, before they are skeletally or muscularly mature, are especially vulnerable to these hazards.

The back is the vital bridge linking the forehead and the hindquarters, while within the rib-cage lie the horse's internal organs. Damage to the back has an indirect effect on the whole horse, so it is far better to take prophylactic measures rather than remedial ones to ensure that the horse remains as sound in this vital part of its anatomy as it does in the others. The horse is only as strong as its weakest link, and the back can easily become that weak link.

I was once teaching at a riding camp where a fat and unfit pony who had been out on both morning and afternoon rides was found during grooming the following day to be extremely sore to touch. It was so sore that the vet was called, and an injection was necessary. The condition was discovered because back inspection was included after every ride and also during grooming. Within one day of this incident, fifty per cent of riders reported that their ponies had shown soreness at different stages of training. The horses and ponies were suffering from over-schooling when they were not fit, but soon recovered after a day's rest.

Fig 63   The rider, taken by surprise, has lost control.

An Ancestral Instinct

When a horse shies it reveals its 'flight instinct', and when it is being ridden the rider's suppression of this instinct may turn the situation into the 'fight' which is the horse's natural alternative.

The human reaction to this equine regression is governed by what the situation involves at the time, which might be highly dangerous if you are on a busy road. However, incidents do arise elsewhere, in places where there is more scope for dealing with the problem.

Some horses are persistent shyers, to the irritation of their owners. The reason may well be in the particular angle of their horse's eye, which affects its vision. It is as well to remember the blind spot in front of the horse caused by his forehead

and muzzle, and the one directly behind. It is also important to remember that when objects appear against a changed background, the horse needs to move its head to be able to focus.

Reversing roles with the horse would make for better understanding of this distracting habit. It is also important to remember that when we lose the horse's attention we also become distracted and lose ours. The horse may well subconciously notice this mental shift of emphasis.

Individual reactions to a shying horse often exacerbate the immediate tendency to control or attack the horse's action, forgetting that the horse's fear is the main thing to be dealt with. If you are riding on a road when this happens, the only hope is to turn the horse's head away from the

Fig 64   Rider keeps his balance and rein contact and remains calm.

distraction and towards the traffic. Pulling the horse's head in the direction of the hazard allows the horse to back off more easily, endangering both your lives as the horse ends up in the middle of the road. When a horse shies habitually, it is obvious that the rider's handling of the situation needs to be examined in a safer setting.

It is important to understand that the horse behaves as it does because of the way it sees certain objects. The ramped retina of the horse's eye means that it needs to move its head to allow the light to fall on it as it tries to focus. If focal length depends on the horse's head position, this provides interesting information for the aware rider. Insisting that our horses carry their heads in a fixed position may not be applicable when it needs a wider field of vision for reassurance. At a more advanced stage of its training, where the horse's head has found an acceptable level, it will naturally become more attentive and confident.

Another strategy which can be used for the shying habit is to work with enough space to allow the horse to move out of range of the object of its terror. This enables the rider to find out the limits of the horse's tolerance.

Confrontation only results in further shying episodes over which the rider has little control. This ends up with the horse becoming even more frightened and the rider even more cross. It is almost as impossible to make a horse approach something to which it has taken exception as it is to make it drink when it is given water. By using tact, the horse can be brought back to a more attentive frame of mind. Once relaxed, it can then be moved gradually nearer the cause of the distraction, which by this time has become acceptable.

In an arena, shying most often occurs in a corner. By avoiding that particular end of the arena, awareness exercises can be resumed and then extended to test the horse's tolerance. When both horse and rider have recovered their concentration, they will usually find that it is then possible to ride past the trouble spot without incident.

The following excerpt, from Lucy Rees' *The Horse's Mind*, sums up the horse's behaviour which we have been discussing, and puts the rider's position in relation to the horse in true perspective.

Gestalt psychologists stressed that an animal does not respond simply to a cue but to a set of conditions of which the cue is only one. 'The whole', they said 'is more than the sum of the parts.' Unlike the American behaviourists, they emphasised the importance of the animal's perception and understanding of the whole situation, or Gestalt. When we fail to recognise a familiar face in an unfamiliar setting it is because the Gestalt, the whole, has changed; when a horse is alarmed at a new arrangement of familiar objects (like barrels lying about a field) it is because the Gestalt is unfamiliar and, when a horse taught to respond a certain way at home fails to do so in a new place, it is again because the Gestalt has changed. Training a horse so that its whole attention is on us means that we become its Gestalt.

5 Partnership

We have now looked at the background of the horse and the rider, and it is now time to evaluate their joint contribution to the formation of a successful partnership. The definition of success is an individual matter which requires personal evaluation, but it really does help to have a clear and positive picture of what you want to achieve.

Fig 65 will help you to assess the qualities which can bring two very different individuals to a point of unison. The arrows at the sides can be extended to indicate the importance of each

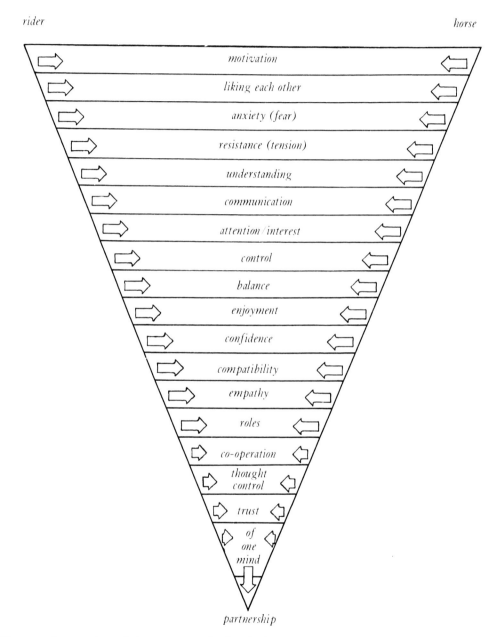

rider   *horse*

motivation

liking each other

anxiety (fear)

resistance (tension)

understanding

communication

attention/interest

control

balance

enjoyment

confidence

compatibility

empathy

roles

co-operation

thought
control

trust

of
one
mind

partnership

Fig 65   An exercise to help you assess the developing partner-ship with your horse.

partner's contribution. This can then be confirmed by marking them out of ten, which should provide some interesting insights.

This project involves both left and right brain activity in the process of asking yourself the questions. While you reflect on your answers your body will become more relaxed because your conscious mind is being channelled constructively, allowing your submerged intuitive responses to surface. You can review your finding at a later stage to assess the progress being made towards mutual understanding between you and the horse.

The project will provide you with the incentive to communicate to your horse something more constructive than a nagging monologue. Dominating the conversation will deaden any interest the horse may have, which you will surely understand if you have ever been the victim of a bore.

To some extent dialogue is an art, which is cultivated for social and business purposes. Why should the same not apply to the horse who partners us, not from choice, but by obligation? In his book *Dressage*, Locke Richards says: 'Once you can do nothing, then you can do something.' We might add: 'and so can the horse'. These words should be engraved on our minds, for when we take the time to listen we will find an increasingly complex equine vocabulary at our disposal, from which horse and rider can learn more about their joint potential.

The horse, with its highly developed senses, is naturally the better listener of the two, and it is this deficiency in ourselves which we need to remedy if we are to enhance our relationship. The more aware we become, the more the horse co-operates, which helps us to extend further the range of communication.

The following extract from R. H. Smythe's *The Mind of the Horse* describes his insights about the human relationship with the horse.

I am confident that the intelligent horse (and it must be remembered insofar as the senses are concerned the horse is far more perceptive than its rider) is capable of reading every thought which enters the rider's mind concerning the matter in hand, and is able to sense every intention, share every thrill, every spot of fear, doubt or loss of confidence which passes through his or her consciousness. It transmits back through the same skin medium, as much as by its actions, its own sensations and feelings, to exactly the same extent as it reciprocates the rider's hopes, intentions and doubts.

Many of the internal obstacles with which we protect our own ego can be removed by a change of thought, which in turn changes the messages relayed by our body. Positive ideas lead to positive actions, which reduce the feeling of having to force the pace due to the fear of failing. When the rider's interest is concentrated upon the horse in the quest for mutual friendship, they are both more likely to relax and open up to the potential which the friendship promises.

Attunement with the horse can become a rich experience, one which the late Captain Edy Goldman has compared with a successful marriage. Before this can happen, however, both horse and rider must move towards a shared sense of inner and outer balance as they work together in circumstances which are not always predictable. With experience, though, it is possible for the horse to make sudden changes in its centre of gravity without disturbing the balance of its rider.

Extreme examples of the horse's ability in this respect are seen in the high school movements, where the horse raises its forehand and springs off its hind legs in the Capriole, or balances on them in the Levade. The horse does not have to be in this class, however, to remind us of its innate ability to stand on its hind legs when it rears.

The closest analogy to riding is probably ballroom dancing, where the man takes the lead and is able to convey to his partner, through his physical nuances, a series of complicated routines. Where the partners are strangers to one another, the steps initiated by the man will be unrehearsed, spontaneous sequences. The partners' responses to one another in dancing are as varied as the responses between riders and their horses.

Reverse turns in dancing involve the same degree of difficulty as changing direction in a riding arena. What makes it more difficult for the horse is that it is the horse that often gets blamed for 'getting the movement wrong'. It is a fact of life that it feels different when you circle in one direction and then change it to the opposite one. Horses who are worked too long in one direction will become disorientated and unbalanced on returning to their natural dominant direction.

Finding the balance with which to move fluently in a right- or left-handed direction requires practice. There is no such thing as perfect symmetry either in horse or human being. Both sides of the body vary in shape and muscle tone. All mammals show signs of having a dominant side: it is not only the horse who is more unbalanced when asked to move in a direction which involves its less dominant side. To experience this sense of awkwardness, try writing with the hand you do not normally use. This is not only a physical concern: it also involves the brain, and, this being the case, both time and patience are more likely to succeed than forcing the pace.

This particular aspect of riding will reveal a further problem for those who cannot readily recognise their right and left hand. This directional sense which most of us take for granted can be devastatingly absent in some people. For them it is an embarrassing problem which they usually try to disguise, but a perceptive instructor will recognise it very quickly. If a pupil takes the wrong turning on more than two or three occasions, a few tactful enquiries will usually uncover the reason. The pupil can be helped, using simple identification exercises for the right and left hand.

Children and adults can both be helped by carrying a red ball in their right hand and a lemon ball in their left hand. This association of letters with right and left provides another clue. Coloured adhesive tape or labels are other options, and ingenuity will suffice when these teaching aids are unavailable.

One of the incapacitating factors for these people is the inability to give directions when trying to explain a route. Instructors need to be particularly sensitive to this difficulty.

Riding naturally means going somewhere, and going somewhere will at some point involve changes of direction. Even riding in a straight line comes to an end at some point, when there must be a change of course. To do this means turning, and, as turns are part of an arc, this leads to the question of riding in a full circle. This is a continuous turning movement until you decide to stop, which brings us back to the clockwise and anti-clockwise directions which we use to help the horses and the rider learn balance. When this balance has been acquired, both will be able to move in any direction and at all paces with the poise and ease of dancers. More detailed information about circles and other movements is given in Chapter 8.

Mobility

Motion is made up of four components: time, weight, space and flow. From these components we can learn to identify our own individual movement patterns. If one of these components is inhibited, it will tend to have a lopsided effect upon our efforts.

Time, for example, can be the component which some people fight against all their lives. Their movements will be quick and jerky, while the movement of someone who indulges in time will reveal a heavier and slower pattern. Time is inevitably involved with a sense of rhythm. If this is deficient, there will be a lack of co-ordination.

Weight is seen in the strength or lightness of the movements used for various tasks.

Space can either open us up or close us in, depending on our personal reactions. Space can be frightening to some people, while to others it represents freedom. The same applies to the space immediately around our body: we can either extend ourselves fully into it, or crouch

down in it hoping not to be noticed. These attitudes will be reflected in our pattern of movement and our sensitivity to those people who invade our personal space. This is also an important consideration we must take into account as we relate to the horse.

Flow is the component which is only made possible as the other three develop. The ease with which you and your horse move your combined weight will involve both timing and spatial awareness. Free flow is more evident in the flexible jump of a cat rather than in the more powerful tense thrust which a horse or deer will demonstrate when they jump, making use of 'bound flow'.

We can now relate the awareness we discussed earlier to the feelings of time, weight, space and flow. Which is the first one to catch your attention and is it related to you or the horse? Remember to keep your attention on the first thing which strikes you and to move to another when you have tried one of the exercises. The chances are that other imbalances may have dispersed during your initial awareness activity.

This information gives you additional reference points for your attention, and will have a bearing on your practical work with the horse when you are riding. Here are some exercises for you to practise in which you will experience reliance on your 'sensing' rather than your sight and will learn how the horse might feel in your hands.

BLIND MAN'S BLUFF

This exercise requires a partner who will lead you around a room or rooms with your eyes shut, helping you to negotiate obstacles safely. If other people are present, see how close you need to be before you sense them. If the floor space is reasonably clear, your partner could move away and let you go solo to see what it feels like.

HAND TO HAND

This exercise also requires a partner, with whom you will experiment with tactile communication. Stand or sit face to face, placing your hands palm to palm, fingers to fingers. Decide who is going to lead the movement: the first partner leads and the other follows. To begin with, stick to leading and following in turns, gaining information and insight as you do so. You can have your eyes open or shut as you wish. Next, try expressing an emotion when you are the leader and see what happens. The more people there are with whom to change partners, the more diversity of contact can be experienced. Some people lead very dominantly, others are difficult to follow; deciding whom you would prefer if they were a horse becomes very apparent. This exercise has had a profound effect on pupils' riding.

SLOW MARCH

This third exercise is for balance. Try walking as slowly as possible without losing your balance. Be aware of your weight as each foot comes to the ground in slow motion. Here you have the elements of time, weight, the space through which you move your feet and body, and the flow needed to keep your balance and rhythm. This is not as easy as it sounds, so alternate the slow march with a brisk one, which will again alter the way you use time, weight, space and flow. Finish by pacing your natural walk. Finally, pretend you are a horse and move your legs and arms in the horse's four-time walk sequence – first your left leg, left hind leg of horse, your left arm and his left foreleg, then your right leg and right arm. You will find that the normal swing of your arms when you walk is not diagonal (opposite leg and arm), but is almost identical to the lateral four-time beat of the horse's walk. The use of two walking sticks held in the hands can make it easier for you to synchronise your timing. Once you pick up this sequence it is rather like watching the two pistons of a steam locomotive and is quite easy to keep going.

This exercise reveals our problems of timing when trying to identify the horse's footfall in walk. By experimenting with your own body you will make it easier to recognise the action of your horse.

Paces

This last exercise leads us naturally to the use and misuse of the horse's paces. Though school movements are part of the horse and rider's training, not everyone has the facilities in which to practise them. All riders, however, are involved in walking, trotting and cantering simply 'to go places'.

The natural paces of the horse can become distorted when it is learning to carry the weight of a rider. Some horses naturally have a better movement than others, depending upon their conformation. Even the most naturally free-moving horse, though, can become restricted by unsympathetic demands. The horse's ability to carry weight depends upon it making adjustments to its centre of gravity which, for a young horse newly presented with an unnatural weight on its back, will put its centre of gravity well over its forelegs. This results in the horse becoming rather like a wheelbarrow running downhill and, with the best will in the world, it will find it hard to slow down and stop. The rider can have an uncomfortable ride during this phase of the horse's development. There is ample evidence of novice horses and riders struggling along in a mutual state of bewilderment and discomfort when they are thrown together as partners.

Deportment

When viewed from the side, the shape a horse adopts when first ridden is often with its back humped up rather like a bronco, just as we would round our shoulders and back if pressure were put on them. If, however, the horse's back is weak, it may do the opposite and become hollow. The humped back is a physical indication of the power with which a horse can punch you out of the saddle when it bucks.

When a horse has good muscle tone, it can carry a rider with less disturbance, though there is naturally an adjustment to be made by any horse who has a rider on its back for the first time. Some horses will spend their working lives with their centre of gravity too far forward over their shoulders. This is because their education ceased once they became ridable. Other horses continue their training and are able, through gymnastic exercise, to regain the beauty of their natural movement.

The silhouette of the trained horse varies considerably from its unschooled counterpart. The former has a rounder profile, giving strength to its back and power to its hind legs. When a horse has a rounded outline from poll to croup it is said to have developed the correct outline, or to be 'round'. Other horses may appear flat like a board from poll to croup, with the nose poking forward, or have a hollow outline with the head held high, the back dipped, and the croup prominent. This results in the hind legs being pushed out behind. Some showjumpers have this outline, creating the excitement which results from evasion of the bit and the rider's legs. These horses are full of the resistance caused by excessive tension.

Having described the various equine deportments, which either enhance or detract from the horse's balance, we now turn our attention to the rider's deportment, not so much thinking about correction as about development of awareness.

Whatever your potential for free movement, you need to maintain a positive picture of yourself in your mind's eye (school mirror or shop window), looking elegant, perpendicular and poised. Put your thinking cap on and search for a few descriptive words which can be your talisman. Pupils I have taught have decided that they wanted to feel tall, light, buoyant, perpendicular, confident. You must choose your own emotive word or words, and rehearse them whenever you have an opportunity.

Another option is to choose someone you admire, then tune into a 'mental video' of them, adding all the details you can think of. These tactics can improve your movement without deliberately having to correct it. Using the awareness exercises, you will be surprised how

Fig 66 A horse with a hollow outline.

Fig 67 A horse with a rounded outline.

Fig 68   Rider looking confident.

realistically you can become the part you choose.

The Horse's Movement

Without our interference, the mobility of the horse is a spontaneous expression of energy, power and speed. How can we utilise these natural talents without losing something in the process?

The answer seems to lie with the horse, which will usually ask us to keep out of its way and to follow and support, rather than suppress the dance it has to offer. The horse will accept its teachers if they instruct in a logical and progressive curriculum, the demands of which are within its scope. It will also accept directions from a rider provided they are comprehensible and the horse is able to obey. Interference starts when the rider is unbalanced, stiff and insensitive to the horse's needs. The barometer of tension needs a weather eye kept out for the development of unexpected symptoms.

Working with the horse and enjoying its truly delightful gaits is one of life's joys, and the greater our affinity with the horse the more likely we are to reap the rewards. Each of your horse's paces, with its own unique characteristics, forms a fascinating mosaic of movement. Each has its own pattern and rhythm and its individual uses. They will change as the horse develops and the rider's training progresses. It is therefore important to protect the paces from unnecessary distortion should the rider become over-anxious or over-ambitious.

The four paces of the horse are walk, trot, canter and gallop. There are variations of stride within each pace which affects the way a horse covers the ground, and in a horse's training these are used as balancing exercises. The dressage horse in particular learns to produce these changes within the paces themselves.

91

THE WALK

The walk is a four-time pace. The horse moves its legs in a lateral sequence, producing a marching pattern. The walk has been called 'the mother of the paces', because it is in the walk that learning most easily takes place. It is calming and there is time for the rider to think about what he or she is doing; the same applies to the horse. It is also the pace used in the early stages of a fitness programme, because the horse can be exercised without loss of condition.

The horse walks in the sequence near hind, near fore, off hind, off fore, except if it stops with one foreleg in advance when it will move the opposite hind-leg when asked to walk forward.

Fig 69   Walk sequence – near hind touches ground.

Fig 70   Near fore comes forward.

Fig 71   Near fore touches ground.

Fig 72   Off hind comes forward.

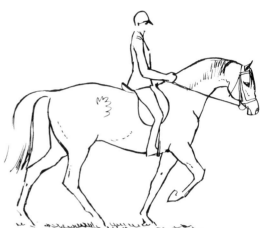

Fig 73   Off hind touches ground.

Fig 74   Off fore comes forward.

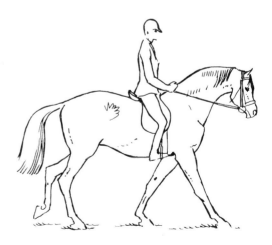

Fig 75   Off fore touches the ground.

Fig 76 Near hind comes forward.

Fig 77 Notice the level of the tape on the rider's right hip in relation to the horse's off hind leg.

It is at the walk that the rider can best experience the feeling of the horse's hind legs coming to the ground, especially if his or her eyes are shut for a few strides, which increases the kinetic feedback. When the rider can relax, the horse's movement gives a lateral sensation, which can travel up the rider's spine with an even more relaxing effect. When the horse feels the rider moving with its own movement, it can then lengthen its walk steps.

The walk pace does, however, have its disadvantages, one of which is a lack of natural impulsion. A horse with a free striding walk is looked on as having an advantage. Because of the horse's tendency to lack this free forward movement, which is of the highest priority in any training programme, it is liable to find itself being constantly kicked along by its rider. Figs 77 and 78 show how the rider's hips are moving with her horse.

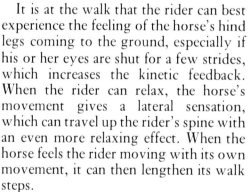

Fig 78 Notice the level of the tape on the rider's left hip as the near hind leg comes forward.

The logic of the signalling system now becomes unstuck, since the rider has changed the conversation to a monologue of 'Go, go, go' at every step. The horse may respond initially, but the next kick comes as a punishment instead of a reward. This makes a nonsense of communication built up on the request, response, reward sequence. If an illogical pattern replaces it, the end result is a totally unresponsive 'switched off' horse. The horse has become defensive, tense and bored, and the rider thinks it is a lazy animal rather than one which is simply confused.

Riders often have more problems with the walk than the horse does, and this is often related to dressage judges' comments about what does and what does not constitute a medium walk. The result of this is that the rider strives endlessly to obtain even more activity from the poor horse, which is already being pushed out of its natural rhythm. This tends to make the walk tense and busy instead of free and flowing.

I have found it interesting to discover that the more aware and relaxed a rider becomes, and the better their body moves with the horse, the longer the horse's steps then become, and the slower the tempo of the beat. These longer steps enable the horse to overtrack with a natural engagement of the hind legs, giving the feeling of power without speed. The horse who maintains these steps with regularity will have found its natural walk rhythm. It is not always an easy matter to help the horse find this rhythm if you are obsessed with the need to produce activity, an obsession to which the horse will usually respond by speeding up its steps at the expense of its natural tempo.

It is the horse's responsibility to walk forward until a new directive is given. If it can only manage a few steps without your constant prodding, accept them with a reward of 'not doing'. Gradually it will walk forward further without support, and will keep going when you remind it to until it develops more and more self-sufficiency. The horse appreciates the dialogue which has helped it to understand what is wanted, but it cannot do this unless its interest has been captured. Having come to this understanding, you will discover your horse is alert and attentive in a way you might not previously have thought possible. The relaxed and easy stride will allow movement with maximum efficiency and minimum effort.

Overcoming the language barrier in the walk pace takes you a long way along the path to true partnership with the horse, laying down a valuable foundation for all the other paces. Though supposedly the easiest of the paces, it can be the pace where much can go wrong in terms of mutual understanding. The walk has an endless fascination for 'aware' riders, many of whom have chosen to spend most of a lesson totally absorbed in their new-found discoveries.

THE TROT

The trot is a pace of diagonal two-time and has a natural impulsion which helps the horse's balance as it moves over these pairs of supporting legs with an easily recognised beat. It is to this beat that the rider times the rising trot. Figs 79 to 82 illustrate each beat as the diagonal legs come to the ground.

The trot is a useful working pace at which to further the horse's physical and

95

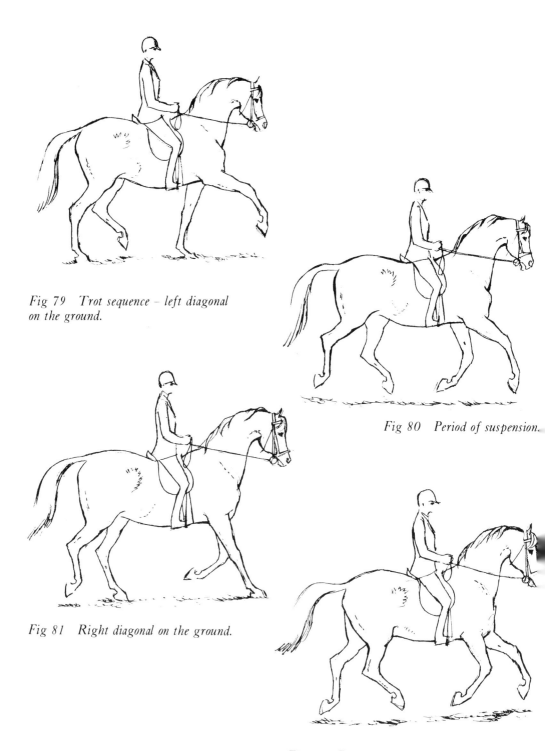

Fig 79 *Trot sequence – left diagonal on the ground.*

Fig 80   *Period of suspension.*

Fig 81   *Right diagonal on the ground.*

Fig 82   *Period of suspension.*

mental maturity. The fact that free forward movement is more readily available gives it a certain animation which both horse and rider can enjoy, providing they can maintain their balance, so it is rightly recognised as a basic schooling pace during which changes of direction, circles, loops, and increases and decreases of the pace itself can be practised.

Each horse has its own natural trot, with which nothing should interfere, any more than we should interfere with our own timing mechanism. Learning to pace ourselves and our horse can relieve the pressures which build up when we persist in going against the flow. At this stage, it is important to appreciate the relevance of each pace to the one above or below it and to recognise the value which changing the pace can contribute to the paces themselves. These changes are known as transitions and they need to be executed smoothly, rather like a good gear change when you are driving your car.

The pace which most frequently comes into its own is the working trot with its natural activity and recognisable beat. It possesses what the walk tends to lack, for all its usefulness. This is where the quest for free forward movement, straightness and rhythm will gain impetus in whatever direction the horse is going.

The rhythmic activity of the trot helps the horse to find its balance, and develops the rider's awareness of fluctuations of rhythm, activity and speed, because they are more easily recognised. The horse, moving as it does in diagonal two-time, has more chance of finding its balance which shows up in even steps and impulsion. Balance for the horse depends very much on forward movement just as it does on a bicycle. The tempo of the developing trot is felt in the regularity of the footfall, and is related to the horse being allowed to move in its natural stride. This regularity, indicative of improving balance, becomes calming and almost hypnotic. Provided there is controlled energy in the steps, the horse will develop an easy momentum which seems as if it could last for ever. As one pupil said when she felt at one with her trotting horse, 'I couldn't tell which was me and which was my horse.'

THE CANTER AND THE GALLOP

The canter is the next pace, but due to its complexity the whole of the next chapter is devoted to its explanation and exploration.

The gallop, which is included in the last chapter of this book, is a pace of four-time, the diagonal beat being divided to give two beats. The same period of suspension takes place after the leading foreleg has come to the ground. The same principles apply to the leading legs in the gallop as they do in the canter.

6 Canter Consciousness

The canter, which is a more complex pace, deserves a whole chapter to itself. It represents varying degrees of difficulty for different riders, difficulties which can be encountered at all levels of training. Many pupils have contributed to the following list. You will probably be able to identify personally with some of them, or be able to add your own ideas.

Personal fears include:

- fear of falling off;
- fear of losing control;
- fear of being run away with;
- fear of speed;
- fear of being bucked off;

- fear of not being able to canter;
- fear of going on the wrong leading leg;
- fear of not recognising the leading leg;
- fear of not being able to maintain the canter;
- fear of falling when the horse cuts corners;
- feeling uncomfortable and not being able to sit down in the saddle.

Technical worries include:

- running into canter from trot;
- the horse raising its head in the transition;
- falling back into unbalanced trot;

- the beat changing to four-time;
- cantering with the horse's quarters to the inside of the track of the forelegs;
- having the horse on the forehand;
- feeling the horse is leaning on the reins;
- the horse losing the roundness of its outline;
- a jerky transition to canter;
- a transition to canter which is anticipated too early by the horse;
- disunited: leading with opposite hind leg and foreleg;
- resistance to the rider's outside leg by kicking;
- the horse not accepting the bit;
- inactive – laboured.

Why, one wonders, should the canter precipitate such a wide range of problems? The answer lies in its increased speed and change of movement, both of which can, often simultaneously, undermine the insecure rider's control.

From the technical aspect, the horse employs a more complex sequence of leg movement in order to utilise this gait. With these variations, which are not always predictable, the rider may feel that he or she has little control. For many riders the canter is the least understood pace, and its successful performance depends not only on an understanding of the horse's problems, but also on being able to cope with the rider's own uncertainties.

The trot, as we have seen, is a diagonal two-time pace, the only variation being seen in trotters who sometimes 'pace' using lateral legs rather than diagonal ones, but the beat is still two-time. The walk does not vary except in unusual circumstances, such as when a horse is pushed to the limits of its stride when the four-time beat seems on the verge of becoming a two-time lateral one. This is seldom seen, however.

The canter is a three-time sequence of legs, with the horse bringing one hind leg forward on the first beat, followed by a diagonal beat of two legs and then the remaining foreleg, which is diagonally opposite the hind leg which precipitated the canter. For example, if the horse commences with its near hind for the first beat, it will move to the off hind and near fore for the second or middle beat, and arrive on the off fore as the last or third beat, after which there is a period of suspension. This gives a picture of the horse rocking from one corner to the opposite corner across the strong middle beat, after which all four legs are off the ground, hence the analogy of the rocking horse. It is the movement which gives the swing to the horse's back, as no other pace can do. If the head and neck of the horse are restricted, though, this becomes impossible, and the lively freedom of the canter is lost.

Other complications which arise in canter are a result of the horse's ability to use whichever leading leg it chooses, until the rider is able to make the decision. Many horses show a preference for one particular lead, and will find it difficult to adjust to the alternative one. This is due to the dominant-handedness we discussed earlier, which influences both humans and horses. Lack of training can make a horse very one-sided in this respect.

Most people will have watched horses cantering, either in real life or in films and videos, and will have realised either consciously or unconsciously that the nature of the canter draws the eye to the leading leg of the horse.

Fig 83   Sequence of legs in canter:
off hind on the ground.

Fig 84   Near hind, off fore.

Fig 85   Near fore (leading leg)
on the ground.

Fig 86   Period of suspension.

The leading leg plays an important part in the horse's ability to keep its balance on a left- or right-handed circuit. In order to achieve this they need to be on the inside lead, a deficiency which is evident in a race horse which can only lead on one pair of legs and finds itself running on a track with the opposite bend. This causes it to lose ground on turns and is the reason why trainers choose tracks to suit their horses. On the other hand, there are certain trainers who teach their horses to be ambidextrous; one such trainer regularly takes her racehorse to my awareness courses.

The horse's state of fitness will inevitably have an effect on its balance, but even a healthy horse will be lacking if it is worked in a lopsided way. This is why it is important for a horse to use its body evenly, by being ridden on both diagonals in the trot and leading with both pairs of legs in the canter.

It represents something of a quantum leap in the horse's ability to understand, through the medium of your signals, which is its left leg and which is the right. The extension of the vocabulary and physical co-ordination needed to do this gives both rider and horse a wider range of control.

Signals from the rider not only ask for forward movement, regulation of pace, and direction, but, given practice, can also position the horse's body for oblique movements. In order to understand the situation in which you put your horse, try the childhood game of playing horses. Canter on your own feet with alternate legs leading. Then try some tight circles

Fig 87   The horse leading with the inside leg round a corner.

101

Fig 88   The horse is leading on the inside leg.

with just the inside leg leading, then try again with your outside leg ahead. This will bring home to you the dexterity required from the horse, especially if it is to do this with a rider on board who interferes all the time.

At a more advanced stage of schooling, it is possible to train a horse to canter round a bend with the outside legs leading instead of the inside ones. This is another quantum leap for our horse's intelligence as well as for its agility. This movement is known as counter canter, and is used to increase suppleness and balance. When the horse is asked to change leading legs while still cantering, this is known as a flying change.

When at liberty horses do often change their lead quite naturally. When a novice horse is being ridden it may do this through loss of balance, which can result in the horse changing the foreleg but not the hind leg. When this happens it is called a disunited canter. It is easily recognisable by the uncomfortable feeling it produces for the rider. This is why the earlier stages of schooling do not include such athletic feats. The lead at this stage is changed by moving into trot or walk, from which the necessary preparation can be made for a fresh canter transition. These are known as 'simple changes of leg'.

During training, the horse must be helped to develop bilateral suppleness, so that what flexibility there is is available with some degree of equality. While we can recognise and accept asymmetry, we must not accept imbalance. The stamina and soundness of a horse depend upon it being able to use the whole of its body.

By this time questions may be arising in the mind of those readers who are not conversant with the canter signal. Just how can these complex signals be given, and how much are they expected to

Fig 89   Counter canter.

remember? This is a common problem, but if you keep your wits about you the difficulties can be avoided. Riders who are overly nervous when faced with the technicalities of the canter only contribute to an increased and unnecessary sense of pressure.

The pace is easier to understand if we begin with the young horse learning to canter. It may have already done so on the lunge and become obedient to a verbal command. Yet the lunge circle is not really large enough for the young horse, so its cantering experience may be limited to when it is taken out for a ride. An older untrained horse can also have difficulties going into canter.

When you understand the complexities which confront the horse when learning to canter, you can reduce the dangers by not building up unrealistic expectations. You can go and discuss your problem and ask for help; the horse has no resource other than an aware rider. Being aware of what is involved when you ask the horse to sort out its left and right sides also increases the horse's awareness of you, which is the point where real rapport begins.

If you ask riders what they are doing when they ask their horse to canter, they will often explain a complicated series of preparations and instructions. Such complexity can easily become a distracting interference for both them and their horses. It is very easy to underestimate the horse's ability to work things out and contribute to the process, if only the rider will sit still and give the horse time. Canter is the one pace where 'thought' or 'intention' alone can provide sufficient muscle stimulus to cue the horse for a change of pace.

Riders will always do better when they actually want to canter, rather than doing it because they think they should, or because they are made to do it. You are half way there if you reach the point of really wanting to have a go. The same applies equally to the horse.

If too much advice is given about how to make the horse canter, you can easily end up trying too hard. It helps to remember that in teaching a horse to canter, we are asking it a question rather than forcing an issue.

Horses like to canter. When they canter in balance it gives them a sense of freedom. On the other hand, and just like their riders, a loss of balance can produce panic. The rider's attention must be diverted from anxieties such as falling off and thinking about wrong leads, and instead set firmly on the horse itself. The rider's whole attention is required for the dialogue with his or her horse, a dialogue which starts by asking the horse a question.

The rider asks the horse if it is sufficiently well balanced to change pace and, if it is, the reply will be yes. If not, it will be no. It is important to accept the 'no' as being the horse saying it is not ready or able to comply, rather than as disobedience or failure. The majority of horses who have difficulties in cantering are not delinquent.

It is the rider's responsibility to create the best possible conditions for the horse to be able to change into the new pace. So what is the horse asking for? In the early stages the horse will be asking for room and speed. Yes, speed, in spite of all instructions to the contrary. The young or untrained horse needs extra momentum (not a restricted trot) so that it can utilise the loss of balance as a means of tipping itself into a canter. This involves increasing the trot until the horse naturally breaks into the new pace.

This introduces the idea to the horse that it can canter. The rider's deliberate use of loss of balance eventually makes it possible for the horse to be able to respond to its rider's command more quickly.

The following story will provide some idea of how the horse learns to co-operate if we avoid overloading it with technicalities.

A four-year-old Highland pony, with very little schooling, came on a course with her rider. Cantering was quite impossible for her on the first two days. However, on the third day she trotted forward to the point where her balance tottered on the brink of canter. The first two days her answer had been, 'No, I can't do it'. By the third day she was cantering quite happily in both directions without the need to increase her trot. Her answer now was, 'Yes, now I know how to do it'. Let us just go over that process again. The rider asks the horse if it can canter by giving the young horse a chance to trot energetically forward until it reaches the point of canter, where it will become apparent whether it can change pace or not. The rider should try this in both directions, because one may be easier for the horse than the other. The rider should use rising trot to increase the stride. This will push the horse sufficiently off balance to put it into canter.

How the horse responds to your request for cantering is a yardstick of its overall development. You are asking the horse if it is physically able to canter. If you find that your horse can canter with the help of some extra input in the trot, you may soon feel that you can achieve it from a working trot.

Having given the signal for canter, sit quietly to give the horse time to react.

You may be surprised at the horse's readiness to do so. Your dialogue might sound like this: 'Can you canter from this trot?' The horse might reply, 'Yes, I can get it and I'd love to canter' or it may say, 'No, I don't have enough energy'. You can of course put your own interpretation to your horse's answers.

Later on, you may feel that the horse has become sufficiently athletic to be able to make the transition from walk into canter without trotting. The readiness of the horse to reply often surprises its rider. Somehow the canter often makes riders so over-anxious that they override, spoiling what can be a most exciting stage in the development of co-operation between horse and rider. Asking questions calmly and sitting still while you await the answers are the secrets of success.

To reach elegance and buoyancy in the canter takes time and patience in the early stages, but the reward gives a renewed stimulus to the horse's increasing aptitude. It is important to establish a well-balanced trot after each canter practice. This consolidates the basic principles of training and provides the horse with a chance to improve the next canter transition. It may take a day or a week or weeks, but it is worth it. Horses have so often been bottled up in their trot while their riders try to make them canter, the rider's explanation being that they thought the horse should not be allowed to accelerate the trot before it cantered. This is true, of course, at a later stage when the horse will strike off into canter without any change in the tempo of the trot.

Always keep your attention on one step at a time: what is it that you want to do next? If the horse has difficulty breaking into canter, helping it to do so must be the first priority, regardless of which leg leads or how fast the trot may be. Once the horse does canter, it can be rewarded, and the seed is sown. Rise to the trot before and after the canter if the stride is long and unbalanced. Reward all responses with rest and reflection: latent learning is more likely if you keep calm and ask for a little at a time. Ride your horse in both directions to develop its overall balance.

As the horse begins to understand, use a slightly different signal when you ask it to canter. Draw your outside leg back slightly, and use your inside leg a little further forward. For example, if you are riding in a right-handed direction you will draw back your left leg slightly and use your right leg a little further forward. Thus, the horse's head is directed over the leading leg. This displacement of the rider's legs will become associated with the canter strike-off, and will later be consolidated in other movements which requires more control of the horse's hindquarters. Making too much movement with the outside leg can disturb some horses and make them tense. It is important to notice what works best for your horse. Each horse's tolerance and interpretation is unique.

Do not try to keep the canter going. If the horse is balanced, it will stay in canter; if not, it will trot. It is far better to start again than to push the horse on. You do not improve the canter by continuous cantering: this simply puts the horse more on its forehand as it tires. It is better to use numerous transitions in and out of canter, and use the other paces to develop the required balance. I once heard the late Captain Edy Goldman advise a pupil who wanted her hunter to canter as

Fig 90 Too much outside leg – note period of suspension.

proficiently as his horses to work on the transitions every day.

Changing the Pace

Transitions teach the horse to adjust its centre of gravity and to pay attention. They can be made progressively from one pace to the one above or below. These are known as progressive transitions, while those which are done by missing out the consecutive pace are known as direct transitions. An example of the latter is seen in making a direct upward transition from walk to canter without any trot steps; reversing the process to come back to walk would require a direct downward transition. The terminology is very similar to changing gear when driving, and the process can become just as smooth as using a synchronised gearbox.

The introduction to the canter is a logical progression of the rider's and the horse's education. Each pace influences the ones above and below it, rather like a scale in music which you can run up and down and use to play a tune. The paces are not always equally well balanced and fluent, and it is important to recognise the horse's strengths and weaknesses in this respect. There is no doubt, however, that a knowledge of the way that paces can be used to enhance each other can make a world of difference to the overall performance. Once the horse has had time to re-establish its balance, the canter can be used to improve the trot, just as trotting, with its natural animation and tempo, can improve the walk.

Horses with a natural aptitude for the canter can use this pace to loosen up before starting work, settling down much more quickly than they would if they were kept in trot. The benefit to the horse's back in canter also makes it a gymnastic exercise, though this will only be possible if the horse is allowed to oscillate its head and neck.

So when the time comes to canter, ask yourself how the idea of cantering affects you. Do you have a major anxiety? Do you worry about the technical requirements? Do you worry about feeling a failure if your horse does not canter? Do you really want to canter? If so, what is it that appeals to you?

Fears and concerns about technical excellence will only obscure the potential pleasure of this pace, so it is vitally important to remain single-minded, realistic and calm.

Here are some 'attention spotting' exercises to help your body to relax. Try carrying a ball, holding it in each hand in turn when making a transition. Then use two balls, one in each hand, when you ask the horse to canter. Notice the horse's ears before the transition, at the moment of strike-off, during the steps of the canter, in the transition down and finally when it has returned to a rhythmical trot.

A pupil of mine contributed the following information when she practised with her own horse, which had a leading leg problem. She tried holding a small ball in each hand. To her surprise there was a pronounced difference in her outside hand when asking for canter, when she had expected to notice the difference in her inside hand. This indicated that she was picking up the middle diagonal beat in her hand rather than the leading foreleg beat, about which we tend to become rather obsessional. This interested her so much that the leading leg problem mysteriously disappeared.

It is tempting to split hairs about the quality of the horse's efforts with comments like, 'The horse was obedient but he ran into the canter' or, 'He put his head up'. The word 'but' always detracts from the initial compliment and tends to turn it into a negative assessment. 'But' is a neutralising word, and shows that the focus of attention is being diluted. The horse may miss out on encouragement as a result.

When the horse is breaking into canter more easily, you can monitor its head as your next priority, but make sure you also use the hand-held balls for this because the problem could easily be your hands or your seat. The balls will help you to relax into the experience, rather than trying to make the horse do something for which it is insufficiently prepared.

The influence of the rider's thought to implement the canter has already been suggested, and its effectiveness has been demonstrated by participants in quiz games such as 'Give us a Clue' or 'What's my Line?' when answering questions. It has been found that they are more likely to reach the right conclusions when the panel can say 'Yes' to the questions posed. This function is known as positive reinforcement. This is the affirmative way to think about the canter. The ultimate aim is to be able to allow the horse to canter, in balance, on a long rein with its head down, neck stretched and back rounded. This achievement cements the trust on which the partnership is built.

Anna's horse found the canter its most difficult pace and had a preference for leading with its near foreleg. This problem persisted through her lessons and her practice at home.

Following up the awareness theme, she decided to ride bareback in her own enclosed outdoor arena. She did this at

Fig 91   Cantering on a long, almost loose rein.

night as her school was supplied with lighting. Her first discovery was the emphasis which the light and the dark had on the two sides of her horse as she moved round the circuit. When she went right-handed, the outside of her horse was in the shadow while the inside was in the light. When she went left-handed, the opposite was the case.

Since then she has become more aware of the shape of her horse when it is on a circle, and now thinks of her horse as having a 'light' and 'dark' side. These have become her key words, and help her to recreate the balance she felt on the night she was riding bareback.

This also improved the canter which she did bareback. In her own words, the horse felt lighter on its forehand, and seemed to have more length in front of the saddle (this particular horse was in fact very short in the shoulder and neck). This interested her greatly and she discovered that she was asking less from the horse because her attention was not on 'doing' but on 'noticing'. As a result, the horse gave her more.

She went to bed that night feeling much less frustrated with herself and her horse, and slept better. She was now riding for her horse *and* for herself, producing the feeling which she describes as 'her becoming the horse and her horse becoming her'. After this experiment the horse had no further problems with its canter.

7 The Coach

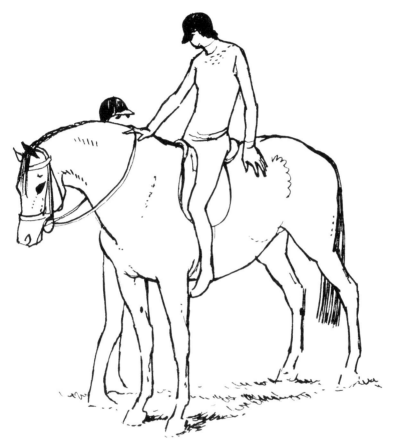

Some years ago, the educational psychologist Joyce Bradshaw wrote about her investigation into what helps learning and what hinders it:

The attitude of teachers determines the attitude of children towards each other and once it is built up it is difficult to break down.

Children quickly learn to feel they are no good from the derogatory comments of teachers, parents and other children. Children pick up ideas about themselves such as 'I am good, or, I am no good'.

Children's reactions to difficulty and failure take many forms: evasion, discouragement, truanting, making excuses, blaming the teacher, boasting that they did not try and genuinely ceasing to try, and seeking success elsewhere, aggressiveness toward other children, bad behaviour in class and delinquency. More mature attitudes to difficulty include continuing to try, the acceptance of inevitable failure and defeat, and redoubling one's efforts in the attempt. Teachers too readily assume that, despite the problems, these last two are the only expected reactions. In fact, the others are much more likely.

If we can encourage our pupils to use all their senses they can learn how to diagnose their own and their horse's difficulties and mistakes. Because they have been intimately involved in the process they are more ready to accept correction, and in many cases it may be possible for them to reach a partial solution for themselves. This leads to increased attention to the task in hand, more awareness and significance of the sensations experienced in riding, independence in thought and movement, and a more co-operative and receptive attitude.

In order to facilitate the learning process, it is necessary for pupils to be actively engaged in the situation in a creative way. This is not limited to the physical movement inherent in riding; it also includes the intellectual and emotional aspects, which are of equal importance.

For many people the word 'teacher' evokes memories of authoritarian school days, and of a pupil/teacher relationship designed to instil fear rather than creativity which the natural riding coach endeavours to adjust.

Should you decide to implement this technique, the main change is in the way that information is exchanged. Instead of the coach being responsible for supplying information, the pupils are helped to find it for themselves. This brings you, the coach, from your side of the fence on to theirs, making you far more accessible to them.

When the coach is setting up a format for a pupil's journey of self-discovery, he or she will supply interesting and thought-provoking routines, rather than technical advice. This needs creative thinking in order to develop new ideas for the pupil's growing awareness, both parties being called upon to utilise their intuitive resources.

The coach will find it stimulating to receive from the pupil first-hand, and often original, information. The horse becomes the checkpoint of progress because it reflects and confirms the pupil's findings, taking on something of the role of referee.

Any coach who has experienced a long day's teaching will find this concept much less exhausting to implement, because the responsibility, the interest and the momentum of the lesson is shared with the pupils. Instructors often complete a day's work feeling as though they have ridden all the horses as well as having tried to improve all the riders. If this is your experience, the role of natural riding coach can be revitalising.

Pupils who rely on being told become passive pupils, and because rote learning has a forgetting rate of two-thirds, it results in constant reminders from the instructor. This only adds to the effort of imparting information, because you also have to din it in. The emancipation of a participating pupil can take the load off a coach's shoulders, enabling him or her to use their expertise for the pupil's greater benefit.

It may seem strange coming round to the pupils' side of the fence, but once everybody has settled down in the new situation, the benefits will soon become obvious.

The first difference to notice will be the pupils' self-confidence. This grows for various reasons, but it starts with the coach's concern for people as people and not just as pupils. This is made clear at the beginning of a lesson when the natural riding coach asks how people feel when they arrive.

Both pupils and coach may find such questions daunting, the pupils because they recall schooldays when they were made to feel foolish, the coach because he or she is learning to use a new technique to replace instruction. It is an adaptive process for all concerned.

Once pupils discover that they can talk freely, it promotes a general sharing of experience which has a supportive effect on everyone involved. A creative dialogue develops as the pupils become increasingly aware, and the process becomes increasingly informative for the coach. The pupils' increasing confidence shows in their ability to investigate their own and their horse's potential. This means that they can move forward at their own pace, rather than at the pace at which the coach thinks they should be progressing.

Though the coach may initially launch an activity, pupils who are evolving their own journey of discovery often take the coach along with them.

The coach will suggest exercises which help the pupils to notice and feel how their thoughts influence their bodies and, indirectly, their horses. This will often involve asking questions which lead the pupils to a focal point of interest in themselves or their horses. This interest is maintained by exercises and games, such as we have explored in Chapter 3. The aim of these ploys is to help the riders to monitor changes from step to step, both in themselves and in their horses. This sensory acumen can be developed to an extraordinary degree, as the riders' ability to relax increases their body awareness or 'proprioception'.

In this respect, the 'numbers game' facilitates numerous changes in the rider as the following story demonstrates.

Numbers Game

Rosemary came for a lesson with an excitable little horse which was giving her considerable problems, caused by the build-up of resistance in the horse, which wanted to dash off, and the effort of trying not to let it do so.

She was asked by the coach to identify what she felt was her or her horse's overriding difficulty at that point in time and how it made her feel physically as well as mentally. Her reply to this question was that she felt anxious and uncomfortable. She was then asked to discover what part of her body felt most uncomfortable, and when it was most pronounced. This turned out to be in the rising trot which was throwing her too high out of the saddle, as the horse was so tense in its back. She was asked to use numbers for the degree of lift which she was feeling. After adjusting her basic balance she commenced the exercise.

First of all, she called the numbers in a high-pitched breathless voice, then with encouragement from the coach to keep calling them out without worrying about their accuracy, she became more interested in what she felt, which reduced her tenseness. The horse, on hearing her voice change to a lower pitch, began to calm down. When this happened, Rosemary's rating of her feelings became more confident and accurate, so that the coach knew she was recognising the change taking place in herself and her horse.

This exercise can also reveal misunderstandings when the numbers being given by riders do not tally with what the coach sees taking place. When the discrepancy occurs, it is advisable to interrogate the pupils in order to discover if their attention has inadvertently been taken up by a new focal point of interest. There is of course no reason why this should not happen, as it is probably appropriate, but the coach needs to know that this has happened and the riders need to understand that they can move their attention as developments demand, providing they inform the coach.

In Rosemary's case, this exercise was applicable to other areas of interest of which she soon became aware. When the rising trot became more comfortable and the lift less exaggerated, she realised this was because she was less tense and had released the horse, which was now more comfortable to ride.

These developments give pupils confidence in themselves, their horses and the coach, which helps them to become more self-reliant and accelerates their progress. The coach will receive confirmation of this by hearing the difference in the pupils' voices, seeing the change in their body language and facial expression and, last but not least, the horses' reactions to what has taken place. This awareness experience leads the coach to trusting both pupils and horses and also to realising the value of keeping mutual attention in the present.

There are many advantages to this simple exercise. It is capable of absorbing a rider for considerable periods of time, and the coach should resist interrupting unless it is absolutely necessary. If pupils are given permission to work on a topic as long as they wish, it is surprising how long they will spend investigating and confirming their experience, proving that normal lessons have far too much content and not enough time for consolidation.

Pupils know much better than the coach how much time they need, and it is often longer than we realise. The coach will notice that the pupils' feedback to questions about their discoveries improves along with their physical progress.

The coach will become increasingly aware of the pupils' interested involvement in their individual projects. This often overcomes the difficulty encountered with pupils who do not listen to what is being said, or who resent criticism. The role of the coach also clarifies, demonstrating the pupils' need for the questions which direct their thoughts to physical sensations and which facilitate attentiveness through the use of awareness games. The feedback this produces provides a powerful incentive for pupils to become even more alert to what is going on between them and their horses.

Increased sensitivity becomes even more apparent with practice, both in the information gleaned from the physical experience and in the way experiences are described verbally to the coach. Diffident pupils become enthusiastic and excited about their discoveries, and their confidence is evident in the way they answer questions and create their own exercises. Relaxed concentration can on occasions turn into total absorption.

When pupils first encounter the natural riding concept the coach must be supportive and allow time for readjustment and time to unwind. With the reassurance that there will be no criticism of mistakes, pupils begin to feel differently about the coach, and soon gain the confidence to choose themes they want to follow up and the amount of time they wish to pursue them.

The following true story shows how such a sequence of events can unfold.

Liza came for a lesson with the reputation of being a difficult person to help. She was a dressage enthusiast with considerable promise but, for some reason, had come to an impasse in her training which seemed to defy resolution.

During the preliminary introduction the coach observed that Liza's body language gave evidence of considerable anxiety. She crouched in the saddle, fidgeted, and spoke in a tight breathless manner, while her horse also looked equally ill at ease and irritable.

When she was asked what had been happening, she described a whole saga of woe, the main factors being conflicting advice, not understanding and ending up feeling hopeless.

'What would you like to happen in this lesson?' asked the coach.

While she paused to think, her body was momentarily still.

'I would like my horse to lower her head and accept the contact of my hand on the rein,' she said more positively.

'In that case, go and ride for a few minutes and notice what catches your attention. Notice the first thing – don't try too hard – then come back,' said the coach to her.

She returned quite quickly, having noticed a stiffness in her back. The coach set up an exercise for her using a scale from one to ten to rate the degree of discomfort. Once more, she was reminded not to try too hard, but simply to notice and grade the feeling every few seconds. Once she overcame the initial strangeness of the technique, and with the assurance there were no wrong or right numbers, Liza became very involved in the exercise.

When the coach called her back, she revealed more awareness of her arms as the stiffness in her back decreased. She said she felt more relaxed.

'Do you notice anything else?' asked the coach.

'No, I was too occupied,' she replied.

The coach then asked her to repeat the process of simply riding and noticing if there was anything different about it now. After one circuit of the school, Liza came back with her answer. 'My horse's head has come down,' she said. It was true: her horse no longer had the giraffe-like stance with which it had started the lesson.

'There is a new feeling on the reins,' said Liza. 'Can I use numbers for that?' This, of course, is what the coach was hoping would happen.

This time the numbers rang out confidently, accurately and consistently, and the horse confirmed the success of the technique with a new relaxed confidence. She did not notice when her husband arrived to exclaim, 'It's great. What happened?'

'Liza has discovered what she needed,' was the coach's reply.

Liza's experience demonstrates the coach's role as being that of a director who organises the sequence of events, such as the pupils' arrival, settling in, introducing the concept, and setting it up for pupils to explore with confidence and safety.

To an experienced coach this will not present any difficulty. The main difference will be the extra time needed to investigate the pupils' states of anxiety and physical tenseness. There will also be more time spent in listening and observing than in talking. The coach acts as a sounding-board for the pupils' discoveries and, in conjunction with the results they produce in the horses, the coach helps to confirm their results. You will also find yourself having flashes of inspiration as your own awareness develops as you coach, and may wonder where they come from. This is your creative ability being given a new stimulus.

To sum up, the natural coach will direct, assess, question, organise awareness games, listen, observe, innovate and demonstrate where necessary. In fulfilling these requirements you will develop a degree of perception which can be of value to everyone involved in the learning process.

Improved Relationships

How pupils relate to the natural coach can be judged from what the pupils themselves have said. Natural riding pupils I have known have seen their coach as a kindred spirit, a friend, an enthusiast, a person who confirms their thoughts and helps them use their initiative, a catalyst, a calming influence, a gentle guiding hand towards something exciting, an ally, a facilitator, a therapist, a supportive guide, someone who helps them to find rapport with their horses, the person who introduced them to a new approach to riding, a co-traveller in the learning process, a confessor, the one who showed them how to decide priorities, someone to be trusted but not worried about, a source of knowledge.

These interesting new interactions between the coach and the pupil also help to clarify the horse's role. The horse begins to make its presence felt in a way that resembles someone coming into its own rights, a valuable member of the learning team. In the last few years I have observed an increasing number of horses being brought to me when they were confused. Such horses often appear to understand the dialogue between me and the rider, and often seem already to have prepared themselves for whatever action is under discussion. This happens without any words of command or names of paces being used, and before the rider has become aware of revealing any physical intention. This seems to indicate that a rider does emanate some muscular change when thinking about intended action. Similar gestures are observed when the rider has made a breakthrough which frees the horse from restraint. The horse appears to know that the coach has been the catalyst. These gestures are seen in its eyes and ears, which express interest and attention. The horse begins to demonstrate a sense of participation in the intervals of discussion and, instead of switching off and looking bored, it is alert, interested and friendly. This may well indicate the horse's appreciation of the benefits and joys of relaxation in which everyone is involved.

Pupils often ask the coach questions relating to the horse such as, 'How much contact do I need on the rein?', the answer to which often lies with the horse itself. When the pupil can relate questions directly to the horse, it responds very precisely. For example, how much or how little you alter something is bound to have an effect on the horse, the result of which can be taken as a yes or no answer. If a signal is too strong or a task too difficult, the balance of both rider and horse will be upset and resistance may arise. In this way, the question is answered easily and gently, rather than by evasion and disobedience. In saying 'no', the horse is often trying to express a genuine difficulty.

A pupil will often ask the coach what length of rein should be used. This is a typical question which a pupil can easily work out with the horse. The same applies to the degree of pressure or tension on the rein, which the horse should be capable of answering in a way that the pupil understands. A positive answer will be one where the horse and rider feel relaxed. A negative answer is one when resistance comes into the picture. By giving the horse a chance to have its say, it is possible to eliminate many of the difficulties produced by expecting too much, too soon, and often for too long.

In this more emancipated role, the horse becomes more interested in the rider, the exercises and the coach. This shows in greater alertness, co-operation and relaxation, and in general expression and movements. The horse's ears are pricked and mobile, and it makes its presence felt as a participant of considerable importance, often with something valuable to say. Seen in this light, the horse becomes the coach's partner as well as the pupil's.

This environment reduces the danger of making false assumptions about each other. Both rider and coach can make such assumptions about the horse, and the coach can easily make assumptions about the pupil.

It is easy to believe that real understanding has taken place when this is not so, just as it is easy to assume that a rider might find a particular horse unsuitable for his or her level of skill but, in fact, get on very well with it. It is only in the openness of debate that these obstacles are uncovered. One pupil I remember had made false assumptions about the medium walk, which she thought her horse should be able to do. This mistake ended up by disturbing all the horse's other paces. It also disclosed her misunderstanding of the judge's comments on her dressage tests.

This, of course, is not a problem which is exclusive to riding. It is a temptation to erect such barriers in other day-to-day activities. Perfectionists can often create problems for themselves by being unrealistic about their goals. A feeling of failure is inevitable in this situation, and assumes exaggerated proportions which are again unrealistic assessments of what is the truth. This naturally produces disappointment, frustration, low tolerance of difficulties and sometimes a feeling of defeat and inferiority. The natural coach can help such pupils to become more relaxed and realistic and, by doing so, can relieve the horse of the demands made on them by a perfectionist.

Humans and animals both need time to learn new lessons, and the coaches too will find themselves learning with their pupils. Anyone in the teaching profession experiences the temptation to cram too much content into a set period of time. Where riding is concerned, everyone expects their money's worth and wants to canter and jump as soon as possible.

This, of course, is an expectation which is fulfilled in many cases, but only at a cost. When natural riding pupils are given the chance to choose the structure of their lessons, they tend to opt for a simple content and spend a lot of time working on it. It is almost as if they go into slow motion as they become kinetically interested in their bodies and their horse. This organic growth of interest is the key factor of any learning activity. It is too often substituted by hectic activity, which fills in the time without pupils really learning what is happening to them.

When a pupil concentrates upon the physical changes they find taking place, the clock often appears to stop. It is not unusual for pupils to pay for private lessons which they spend simply walking, totally involved in sensing where their body is in space and the muscular activity which holds it there.

A coach, finding himself or herself in this situation for the first time, may well feel embarrassed and redundant, and may think that the pupils are having a poor run for their money. The first time this happened to me, no one was more surprised than I was when my pupil dismounted smiling happily and saying 'Thank you, that was a wonderful experience'.

We are constantly reminded about false assumptions by what pupils say about their learning progress. Perhaps we have got it wrong when we think that pupils need to be active continually in order to enjoy themselves. After all, it depends on what is motivating them and where their goals lie. There is no doubt that an active ride tends to exhaust the horse unnecessarily, and can often be seen as a waste of everybody's energy. The great art of coaching is to create interest. If you can do this without a lot of talking, the pupil has a chance to concentrate and learn easily.

One ten-year-old pupil was practising the numbers game while riding her pony. She was very busy and absorbed doing circles when her mother interrupted the lesson, causing the child to become extremely upset.

'Oh, Mummy,' she said, 'why did you do that? I was just going to give my pony an eight.' Adults feel equally irritated when they are distracted by extraneous advice. There is a time and place to cue the rider, but silence is often even more useful. Deciding when each is appropriate is part of the tact which a natural riding coach must learn to use.

Class Size

Class lessons which consist of a number of pupils can include people who vary considerably in their range of standard, as well as in the actual numbers of pupils involved. Commercial viability may sometimes raise the number of pupils to an unsatisfactory level as far as constructive teaching is concerned. The ideal number of riders depends on their ability, the size of the school in which they work, and the level of training of the horses. Sometimes four riders can get in each other's way; at others, six will interweave individual exercises or work as a ride with excellent use of the available space.

In the interests of safety, most schools require horses to be worked in single file, each horse keeping at least one horse's length from the one in front. This control is of vital importance in any class, and is one which is not always put into practice as efficiently as it should be. In fact, it poses considerable difficulty at the beginning of a lesson when pupils and horses have not had time to settle down and concentrate.

Teaching riders to keep the correct distance between each other often results in constant reminders from the instructor, a sure sign that some pupils are still in the passive learning phase. Maintaining correct distance is a far more complex operation than it might seem to be on the surface, for it involves judgement of pace and distance, often before riders have the ability to control their horses.

Tape Exercises

Natural riding can turn this problem into an awareness exercise by sticking a strip of tape on each rider's back. Everyone except the leader then has a primary focal point for their attention. To overcome the leader's problem, everyone takes it in turn to lead. Each member of the class is asked to watch the tape as they ride round, and to remember anything they may notice. This creates immediate attention and more active participation. When the ride is turned into the middle of the school for a rest, riders can be asked about their discoveries.

This exercise works well at pony club camps, and the bored expression on pupils' faces as they listen to yet another homily on distance-keeping disappears as the tape is attached to each of them in turn. The arousal of interest is often quite dramatic, and so are the results produced by this exercise.

When larger classes are being taken, the games may need to be more general in order to get the ball rolling. They may have to be played in class formation due to limited space. However, the discussion which follows will usually provide the coach with individual information from which each pupil can make his or her own adjustments.

A variation on the tape exercise is to stick it on one of the prominent muscles of the horse's neck, and ask each pupil to watch that once they are capable of keeping their distance. This creates interest, helps riders to relax and provides a talking point once the exercise is over. It is from this pool of information that the coach can extract the next exercise, either for the class as a whole or for each individual rider. As the lesson unfolds, the coach can begin to hand over the choice of topic to the pupils themselves.

Tape can also be used with constructive results on the rider's toe, on the saddle in front of the knee, on the top of the hand, on the rein, or the horse's shoulder when teaching diagonals, and other places which suggest themselves to you or the pupils. (*See also* page 48).

Asking the Right Questions

It is important to reassure pupils that your questions are non-judgemental. It is very easy, for example, for a pupil to comment that an exercise feels better, but what exactly does 'better' mean? Having to think about what actually made it feel better helps the physical process of consolidating the result. 'That was awful' is another comment which is meaningless on its own. By asking the pupils what happened and obtaining a factual response, a useful experience is gained. Deciding what needs further attention is then the pupils' choice, a choice which the coach should accept.

Each rider may end up working on an individual theme, without getting in each other's way or needing constant instruction. There may be longer intervals of discussion, which rests the horses and activates the riders' mental faculties. They can all share in such discussions, finding support and encouragement from each other. As they progress they may be able to work individually instead of in a ride, providing they work on the same rein until they prove able to choose their direction without the dangers and distractions of interception. The ball game can be used by a class in the same way; if you do not have sufficient balls to go round, the pupils can work in pairs and watch one another. This also works well with the numbers game, where the participants learn to see what is happening to each other.

This leads to the point where friends can help each other when a coach is unavailable. It is not necessary for one rider to know as much – or more than – another. The most important ability is to be able to ask the right questions. They can either use questions which the coach has asked them, or their own.

Innovation is the successful natural coach's *pièce de résistance*, but pupils, too, often have ideas of their own as they develop a creative approach to improving their performance. As a result, the whole process becomes enjoyable, informative and physically less arduous. As the confidence of rider and horse increases, so does their ability to become aware of the space around them and their new physical sensitivity.

To recap, the following guide-lines should be kept in mind by the natural coach:

• Question rather than teach – provide information and demonstration when asked.

• Explain there are no right or wrong answers, rather different ideas and experiences.
• Learn to be non-judgemental in this respect.
• Give suggestions which lead the pupils' attention to where it appears to be needed, but do not force their adoption if the pupils seem reluctant, as this is to get them started.
• Try to avoid interrupting pupils who are absorbed in an exercise.
• Check that 'trying too hard' has not crept into the situation.
• Check the pupils' focus of attention to discover if it has begun to include more than one topic.
• Trust pupils to choose their own area of attention and time will prove that they are mostly right. If not, let them change to another point of interest.
• Learn to trust your pupils' choice even when you feel it may be the wrong one.
• Learn to trust the evidence which the horse reflects, and also yourself in this new role which may at times leave you feeling redundant.
• Accept the proof provided by the feedback from the pupils that you are providing an important function in their learning experience. Listen to your intuition and notice how it increases in this environment.

The Pupils' Reactions

Pupils have contributed their side of the story by admitting to a high state of tension in an unknown situation and that, even before a ride, tension exists on most occasions, for a variety of external reasons as well as lesser related ones. They do say that the feeling is relieved by showing it and by being able to identify its physical location.

There is continued evidence to support the pupils' need for more time to pursue and consolidate their aims, and that too much content in a lesson is confusing. Sometimes the theme practised in different directions and situations will hold pupils' attention for the entire time. This goes to reinforce the dictum that one thing at a time is conducive to learning without stress.

This factor is related to pupils learning to pace themselves, which leads them to being able to pace their horses with a better understanding of their needs. This is the meaning of doing something in your own time and is often heard in a riding school as preparation to a change of pace, direction or exercise. Perhaps this will be more significant and reduce the temptation to force the pace by overloading pupils with instructions.

When pupils are tailoring their own lesson theme, it will be found that their primary interest, while holding their attention, can lead to the resolution of other discrepancies in the overall picture. This means they have intuitively picked out the main problem. One step in the right direction leads them to other sequential ones as they progress, and, although initial progress may, of their own choosing, seem to be a slow process, it can provide quicker results in the long run. The pupils in this situation know that interest and hectic activity in a riding lesson are not synonymous.

Here are what some natural riding pupils have said about their experiences:

• 'A more sensitive and relaxed approach.'
• 'One can help oneself and each other regardless of individual ability.'
• 'I understood the way the teaching worked with the absence of being told to do this and that.'
• 'I found it enormously beneficial and a complete foundation for the enjoyment I now find in riding. I was seriously thinking of giving it up as I had no confidence and was confused and not enjoying the horses at all. This has changed.'
• 'The positive approach is to look for a good result in every situation.'
• 'I learnt to know when I was hindering the horse.'
• 'I overcame the wish to show off.'
• 'I never thought my horse could be changed after being so tense and excitable for many years.'
• 'I have found it easier to cope with stress.'
• 'Enforces rapport with the horse as with a person.'

This summing up of salient factors which arise in a coaching session must include contributory information provided by the horse, which is after all the mirror of the rider and as such provides the coach with the true situation.

The Horses' Reactions

The horse will confirm the physical and mental attitude of the rider and the coach, and develop its own awareness, recognising the subtle changes which take place during the numbers game, for example. The horse acts as a barometer for the accuracy of the rider's awakening sensitivity.

The horse can, of course, not only reflect the pupil's tenseness but also will exhibit its own symptoms of discomfort if its saddlery does not fit correctly or there is stiffness in its back. It is important to discriminate between the effects a rider can have on its body and its own deficiencies or unsoundness. In this way, the horse is telling a story all the time it is under observation.

The coach needs to prevent the horses from becoming scapegoats for the pupils' problems, though this is less likely in a natural riding situation. Instead, the coach acts as a catalyst through which the pupils search for information and answers, so the relationship between rider and horse becomes more positive. The coach may well find himself or herself included in the situation, as the horse also seems to become aware of the coach's new role which gives it security and interest, especially during the interludes for discussion.

It is not only the facial expression of the rider which changes when relaxation takes place, for the horse's expression changes and his whole body can take up a round soft outline which includes voluntary acceptance of the bit. This is the horse's way of affirmation, of giving himself in total trust.

The following story illustrates the way a horse can change its whole outlook. Rupert belonged to a demanding owner who enjoyed participating in all areas of equestrian competition. On this occasion, a lesson was in progress in preparation for a showing class. The horse looked dull and uninterested, as was often the case, and lacked the sparkle needed to catch the judge's eye. The coach suggested to the rider that he should watch the horse's ears and report on what was happening. After one circuit there was a change in the laid-back angle at which the horse habitually carried

them. Gradually, and much to the coach's surprise, more and more mobility was discerned. The rider returned to discuss what he had noticed. He had observed precisely the changes seen by the coach.

'What were you doing?' the rider was asked.

'Oh, nothing,' he answered. 'I was just watching. But now I see that it was actually doing nothing which changed Rupert's ears. I so seldom do nothing.' This, of course, was exactly what the horse was trying to tell him!

No one process will suit everybody, and it is up to each one of us to choose the method we find most compatible and successful. Coaches must accept they cannot please everyone all the time. What they can do is offer options and make sure they are open to new ideas. After all, it is what works that matters.

In conclusion, here is an answer given by an experienced pupil to the question 'What major discoveries or developments took place in this learning environment?'

'What I have learned,' she said, 'is that there are many doors in your mind waiting to be opened, but you need help and guidance. Your self-image is vital to the way you relate to your horse. The friendship of a horse is a very humbling thing, and must be treasured and protected at all costs. To train a horse or a person and remain their friend is a difficult task – it needs a lot of thought. It is hard always to be fair, but you must do your best, and your attitude helps towards that. You must have control of yourself before you try to control a horse. People need to talk to each other more. People need to listen to each other more. If you are happy, you ride well. There is always tomorrow.'

8 Shapes and Spaces

The successful equestrian partnership becomes evident in the increasing fluency with which the horse moves. This quality becomes an integral part of the horse and rider's overall performance, not just a bonus for the experienced competitor but a harmony which the less ambitious rider can also enjoy.

The word 'harmony' means 'in agreement with', and a harmonious performance is both pleasing and consistent. Harmony in music means notes which produce chords, a pleasing effect of an appropriate arrangement. Underlying a state of harmony in riding is the blending of the rider's and horse's energies, the natural flows which are the basic rhythms of life. Tuning in to these innate patterns helps the horse to reclaim its inherent movement potential. When this happens, horse and rider move with natural ease and unison, while the horse will be able to keep a consistent tempo in all its paces.

When conceived of as an expressive

musical composition, a fluent and harmonious dressage test can be far more satisfying than a more precise and lacklustre performance. A horse which has acquired this degree of balance and freedom will also have increased its powers of endurance, for it will be using energy economically and finding acceleration and deceleration easy to handle. By developing harmony and fluency in your riding, and with a positive relationship with your horse, you are well on the way to wherever you want to go.

Wherever you want to go in exploring your riding potential will involve the use of space. Many more people now have the chance to use indoor and outdoor arenas, but other riders still have to make do with other alternatives for their schooling sessions. This can sometimes be very difficult when no flat area is conveniently available for the riding of basic exercises.

What does space mean to you as a rider? Is it a welcome sense of freedom, or a frightening expanse where all sense of security vanishes? Riders who have started their riding indoors have to be weaned gently from this safe environment, and when they move into an outdoor arena they often feel nervous to begin with. As each step up is taken into a larger space, riders may well encounter apprehension until eventually they find the confidence to work in more wide open spaces. When training students for their British Horse Society exam, I have to help riders who have started in the indoor school to develop their confidence gradually until they have the skills necessary to ride in the hunting field or to compete at one-day events.

Where the horse is concerned, space is a different matter. Open space is its natural environment and, when suddenly presented with it, it can often go to its head. The sudden sense of freedom can prove too much, and it is important that a nervous rider and an excitable horse are not thrown together in this situation.

Your own enjoyment of riding is related to your spatial awareness, too, for when we look at all the equestrian activities now available, riding offers a wide choice of interest in this respect. Whatever your choice as a rider, the horse's kindergarten and primary school education is facilitated if some of it can take place in an enclosed area, and the time spent there will enhance your enjoyment and extend your options. By working in an arena it is possible to gain more control and attention from the horse, and it gives the rider a greater sense of security.

Later you may choose to extend your horse's education to grammar school or even to university level, but it is in the schooling arena that training begins. This is where a horse learns how to change pace and direction, and to become obedient and attentive to its rider's signals when slowing down, increasing the pace or stopping. It is these routines which increase the horse's power of propulsion and its ability to change its centre of gravity, and which help it to become more supple.

These exercises require an extension of the horse's vocabulary, and of the rider's appreciation of what the horse is physically capable of doing. This puts extra demands on the rider's equestrian tact and physical awareness. During these shared experiences space and shape become interwoven. As they use the arena to ride shapes not unlike those seen in figure skating, both horse and rider improve their deportment and work together on the details of the exercises.

A few years ago I had been showing a horse successfully at the local agricultural show. After the judging a friend suggested that I join her in the gymkhana games. Somewhat reluctantly, I agreed to compete alongside the rather boisterous competition, consisting almost entirely of young farmers and their friends. To my amazement I won every event, entirely due to the suppleness and obedience of my horse, which thoroughly enjoyed the experience. This illustrates the wonderful versatility and *savoir-faire* of the horse which, with patience, logical training can produce.

Exploring all the things you can do together with your horse on a long-term basis is much easier if you spend some time paving the way in easy stages. This involves practising in an area forty by twenty metres (forty-four by twenty-two yards) or more (preferably not less), learning the shapes of directional changes, the size of circles it is possible for your horse to perform, and the loops which you can ride to take you round on the opposite track.

The rider needs to understand what is involved in the horse's ability to balance itself, and so be able to follow a direction set by the rider. The rider needs a mental map of all the permutations of directions possible within a limited area. This map, however, is not always available or clearly understood, and it is for this reason that shape, space and direction are explained more fully.

Changing the Rein

We start with the different ways of changing direction, because it is not only horses which have problems in executing them with accuracy. Riders can also become disorientated and lose their way. The arena can be used in a bewildering variety of shapes and directions, and it is easy for a coach to overestimate a rider's competence to memorise them. What is needed are helpful signposts to point the way.

To begin with, ride your horse round the outer track of your arena or schooling area, and consciously watch yourself turning the corner at each end of a straight side. To go round a school once involves four turns in order to arrive back where you started. The turns at each corner are part of a circle: for the young or less supple horse this circle will have a radius of about fifteen metres (fifty feet), while a trained horse will be able to turn a ten-metre circle (thirty-foot).

All changes of direction involve moving through part of a circle – an arc – in order to make the connection between two straight lines. The pace at which the horse is travelling also alters the size of the arc. When you want to go round the school in the opposite direction, you will need to follow the path which is easiest for your horse. The easiest place for the horse to change rein is after the second corner of the short side of the arena. This presents it with a gradual curve which takes it diagonally across the school, to meet the track at a gentle angle before arriving at the first corner on the short side at the opposite end of the school. Changes of rein can be ridden across the school and down the centre, but are more difficult because each turn is really a corner, and the straight lines are harder for the horse to follow without wandering.

The diagonal change can, in error, be

123

taken from the first corner of the short side of the school, making a tight turn which can only be accomplished by an elastic horse. The same restriction is faced at the opposite end of the diagonal. This is not an uncommon mistake, one which sometimes happens in dressage competitions in moments of mental aberration. This is just one instance of losing your way in a small space which can easily seem like a maze if too many routines pile up one after the other.

This, of course, is a rider problem. The rider, being the skipper, needs to plot the course accurately, thus providing a sporting chance of arriving. But the horse can have problems too. The biggest problem is usually that the horse finds it hard to keep its balance while tracing the shape of the track it is expected to follow. For the precise execution of a twenty-metre (22 yard) circle the horse requires the balance of a figure skater. It also finds going down a straight line a wobbly procedure, as anyone who has ridden a young horse will have found out. The wandering, rudderless sensation which accompanies such a loss of control is very obvious.

When riders are practising they do not always understand where they are supposed to go or why. As the routines become more complex, tension begins to mount with the demands that are being made. Once the rider becomes unclear, anxiety levels rise because too many things are trying to be remembered at once, with the result that none of them receives sufficient attention.

Two questions arise when using space. One is knowing where to go, and the other is being able to bring this about. The two, however, are not synonymous. This is where the coach needs to give very clear instructions, and check that the pupil understands what is being asked. Again, awareness games and exercises can help, focusing the rider's attention on the experience itself, rather than on the negative responses which errors can easily provoke. For example, where the rider is unsure which corner is the one to be used to change direction, they can be allowed to experience turning off the track at the first corner, and then at the second. Questions can then be asked about what the rider noticed on each occasion, and which turn felt easier for them and the horse. This procedure helps to eliminate any further likelihood of getting lost or becoming worried about it happening again.

Riding a Circle

Circles provide a shape round which much of the horse's physical development depends, owing to the demand this exercise makes on its inside hind leg in terms of balance and impulsion. By working in both directions, each hind leg can be activated in turn.

While doing these exercises the horse should be calm, for a calm horse is relaxed and attentive. The horse should be willing to go forward when asked to by its rider without becoming over-keen and taking a stronger hold on the bit, leading to restraint. The horse's body should be straight in relation to the line being travelled. This requirement can be explained by the analogy of a train, which follows the rails on both straight sections and on curves, any deviation from which would derail the train. For the horse to be in balance, its hind legs must track directly behind its forelegs whatever line it is taking. Practising a combination of school figures will in time produce all these qualities, which in turn will increase the pleasures of riding in whatever directions it may take you.

It is very useful for a rider to be able to imagine what a twenty-metre (22 yard) circle looks like. This can be a problem when you ride it in the arena, and can be even more pronounced if you have to work in an open field with the minimum of points of reference.

I evolved the following exercises to create the circumference of a twenty–metre circle at a pony club camp, where both space and equipment were at a minimum. Four cone markers were set out at a radius of ten metres (eleven yards) from a centre cone, dividing the circle into four equal parts as nearly as possible. Four more cones were then placed outside the first four, with just enough space between them for the riders to pass.

The measurements were not very precise at first but, as the riders became more aware of the number of steps the horses were taking in between each tangent, the markers were adjusted. The horses gradually began to adapt to the bend of the circumference with little effort, even though not many of them had had any previous schooling of this kind. It was necessary to limit the time spent on this exercise with unfit horses, but rest periods were created by dividing the ride and letting the spectators see how many different-sized circles could be ridden round the cones.

The exercise proceeded like musical chairs. The cones were gradually removed one by one, proving that the horses became more self-supporting as time went by. This turned out to be a most constructive use of equipment, far

better than the four corner markers so often provided at rallies which are virtually useless in terms of geometric precision, and serve only to designate each instructor's schooling area.

The most accurate and easy method of planning a circle is to hold a lunge rein or rope while someone else holds the other end as if they were a horse, and tracks the desired circumference. When this was organised by the pupils themselves, it really imprinted the visual and sensory perception of the circle.

Later, there was yet another improvement to the exercise, involving the use of eight poles to make up a cross, two poles being used for each arm of the cross, with a space in between them to form the required radius. Cones were then used opposite the end of each pole, again leaving a gap through which the horse and rider could pass. This is even more precise, because the right angles between the poles divided the circle equally in four. When this exercise was tried out, one rider asked for cones to be placed between the arms of the cross to identify the circumference. This illustrates the importance of the pupil's participation in the design of the circle, for all could now see that where the tangents impinge on the track there is a danger of being carried along it with straight steps instead of continuing the circle.

This apparatus provided many permutations. Smaller circles could be ridden through the gaps between the two poles, either in walk for the novice level or in trot as the horse became more athletic. Even walking over the poles created a useful exercise for both horse and rider. The rider's sensory involvement in seeing the shapes required and feeling them physically in practice produces a much

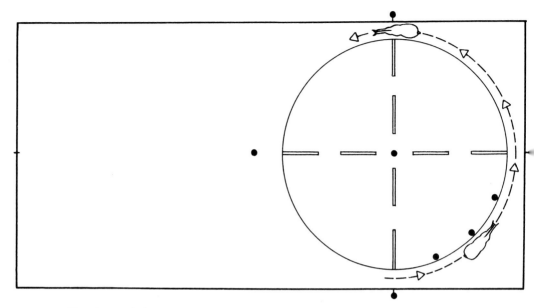

Fig 92   Planning a circle.

Fig 93   Riding round the poles.

more reliable, visual and physical memory than the superficial guessing of an abstract figure.

The first time the plan was introduced it kept one pupil, who had never ridden a circle before, involved for most of the lesson, with very useful results. When he returned a week later there was no call for this support, as riding a circle was now possible without it.

Pupils of the late Captain Edy Goldman maintained that if they could ride a circle which came up to his standard of perfection they could pass muster anywhere. His training certainly produced wonderfully balanced and well-trained horses. He marked the quadrants on the school wall with a cross where the circle met the track and, to illustrate how the horse's head arrived on the track first, he put another cross to show where the head should arrive. As the horse came onto the track the rider's body would be opposite the middle cross, at which point the horse would be leaving the track again. This point is where the third cross was put. When the pupils saw this on the wall, they could appreciate how the end crosses indicated the horse's length. This made them aware of the length which the horse occupied, and prevented the circle being spoiled by inadvertently going down the track with straight sides. This exercise employed the pupil's visual sense, their proprioception, and their hearing as Captain Goldman shouted 'on' and 'off' at each point of the compass. This exercise goes a long way to explaining why his pupils rode their circles with such consistent accuracy.

Once you can ride a circle in this way it is very much easier to ride a straight line with the sureness of an arrow in flight,

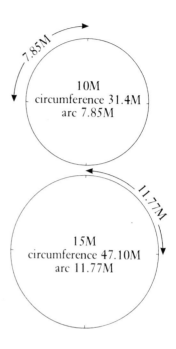

Fig 94 The arc measurements of quadrants.

thus proving the degree of control you and your horse have achieved.

Children are often more bewildered than adults when these exercises are encountered for the first time, and for a small child all the variations of loops and circles must be difficult to perceive. As children in a class often ride blindly one behind the other with only the leader understanding where they are going, it is not surprising that confusion arises. Pupils enjoy the serpentine exercise, for example, once they understand it, but it is unrealistic to expect riders to understand where they are going unless the coach is very explicit. Blind copying without understanding arose at a pony club rally, where a group of children had spent an

127

afternoon riding the serpentine manoeuvre. When they joined a new
instructor, it quickly became obvious
that they did not really know what they
had been doing. The answer was to mark
the loops with cones, so the path they
were taking became quite clear. Cones
were placed on the centre line of the
school where they crossed it, so the way
they should go became obvious. Each
rider took their turn as leader, so before
long everyone understood what they had
been trying to do earlier on.

As you experiment with exercises like
these, the increasing aptitude which you
and your horse will acquire in terms of
balance, agility and control will gradually bring the feeling of actually having
more space and time. As one competitor

remarked after she had allowed her horse
to slow down to its natural tempo, 'I now
feel I have lots of room in the arena and
much more time to think what I am going
to do next.'

As progress brings about more
demands, it is easy to start trying to
spread your attention in order to produce
correct results, so it is good to remember
the awareness principles which keep you
in a state of relaxed attention.

Horses may have difficulty in deport-
ing themselves on an even keel. This
sometimes results in them taking their
corners rather like a motorbike, leaning
inwards as they negotiate the bend. The
horse needs to learn to negotiate corners
using centrifugal force (the wall of death
principle), which keeps them more

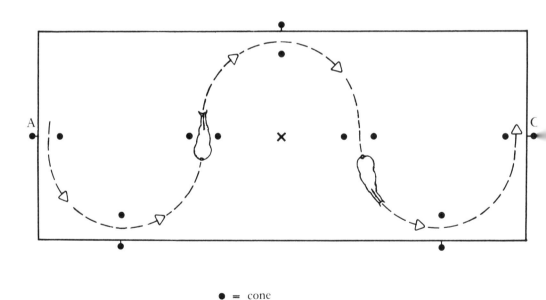

● = cone

*Fig 95   The serpentine: how cones can define the track of this
exercise.*

upright, pressing against the rider's outside leg and rein which act for support as a 'wall'. Lack of straightness means a loss of vertical balance, which displaces the hindquarters or the forehand as they try to compensate. This gives the rider the sensation that the horse is falling about in a way that makes it difficult to steer.

This situation disturbs the rider just as much as the rider who does not sit centrally will disturb the horse's balance. It is important for the rider to be aware of this, even though feeling out of alignment is not easy to detect without the help of an observer on the ground.

Leg Yielding

Up to now, the horse will have been moving forward from the rider's legs and we have now come to the stage where it needs to understand the application of one leg only. Using one leg says to the horse, 'Move over'. When the horse understands this request, it will put the hind leg on the same side as the signal further underneath its body, so that it can take the thrust to push itself obliquely and forward at the same time. The first time this question is asked the horse, being unable to count, naturally tends to increase its speed. 'Legs,' it thinks, 'means faster', so the rider's hands need to restrain this impulse with tact, saying 'No, not faster'. With practice, this combined signal will divert the forward thrust to a more oblique, slightly sideways impetus. Do not be disappointed if the horse has difficulty understanding and co-ordinating its response on its less dominant side, for it will be less sensitive there and thus less well orientated.

Once the message begins to be understood, it will be easier to keep the horse's head in the direction of the track which it is following, including corners and circles. Helping the horse to conform to the arcs and straight lines along which you are travelling is not easy and, when the horse fails, it is tempting to steer on the outside rein. When it cuts its corners this happens all too frequently, but using the outside rein only accentuates the loss of balance. By turning the horse's head to the outside in an effort to hold the horse up, you will only increase the weight on the inside shoulder and make it more difficult than ever for it to recover its balance. This experience links up with the reactions of the horse when it is shying, and this understanding may begin to connect other incidents that arise in your schooling.

The lesson of the inside leg is a vital link in the balancing process of the horse, but it tends to make riders try too hard. In doing so, riders may tend to displace their own weight and block the message they are trying to convey. Making too much effort with your inside leg tends to move your body weight in the opposite – unwanted – direction. The movement you require from the horse then countermands the order you are giving.

To help the horse to understand, proceed in the way you did for canter by asking first if the horse understands and can do it. You will soon know by its response. The easiest position for the horse to learn this lesson is to turn onto the inside track of the school or, if you are riding on a road, a little bit away from the side of it. Keep the horse's head straight and gently nudge it into the outer track, where you want it to go anyway. If you are on the road, nudge the horse with your right leg to push it to the left. As

Fig 96   The horse looking the way it is going on a corner.

you will need to do this on both sides, road users will need to find a quiet track to ensure that moving from one side to the other is reasonably safe. It can help to introduce this idea to the horse in the stable, by asking it to move over when you nudge it with your hand in the same place as you would use your leg, just behind the girth. You can also give your horse a reminder when you are leading it in hand before you mount.

One pupil who was interested in improving her performance in the turning and circling exercises was observed by the coach to be leaning inwards as she worked. She was asked to notice what she did during the exercises, and made the interesting discovery that she tended to

Fig 97   The horse looking away from the direction of travel and falling in.

Fig 98   The rider's outside leg is too far back, causing his weight to move left.

contract her body on the inward side. She decided that it was triggered by setting her jaw as she began the exercise. This information released the tension, and allowed the turn to be made without any loss of balance.

The rider's inside leg creates impulsion, while the outside leg controls the hindquarters and helps to keep them in line with the forehand, or positions them in lateral or sideways movement. This means that different parts of the rider's body relate to specific areas of the horse, providing a sophisticated signalling system which can produce a combination of elegant and flowing movements that are a joy to the rider and a pleasure to watch.

Awareness exercises also contribute to relaxation, without which there is no such thing as suppleness. One exercise which helps when practising circles and corners is shutting your eyes for as many steps as possible, in order to heighten the sensation of riding an arc. Another is to count the steps for both halves of a circle. Marking a particular sensation out of ten can also help to confirm it or to reduce it, depending whether it is of positive or negative value. Try carrying a ball or balls in your hand to check the feeling on the rein. Some people have found that this helps to sense what the horse's hind legs are doing.

The Rein

There is also a rein-release exercise which adds to the vocabulary of signals, and can

Fig 99 Surrendering the outside rein.

provide useful feedback about the state of balance which exists between you at any given time.

This exercise involves slowly pushing the inside or the outside hand forward, as if about to throw a ball, towards the horse's ears. This results in a momentary loss of contact on the rein. When the outside hand is doing this, it releases undue tension on that rein, perhaps caused by the rider holding the horse out of the circle instead of achieving a response from the use of the inside leg. It suggests to the horse that it is free to turn its head and, whether it does so or not, will provide clues to the tenseness of the rider's arm or the stiffness of the horse.

Once the horse has established its balance on a circle, the inside hand can be used in a similar way, counting one, two,

to complete the movement. There should be no loss of bend on this occasion, only the sensation of the horse travelling centrifugally on the outside rein as it remains looking in the direction of travel. When this happens it confirms the horse's stability and suppleness. This movement provides instantaneous relaxation for both horse and rider, and restores harmony in the horse's mouth, as well as becoming another method of reward. In fact, it gives such a pleasing sense of gracefulness that riders may tend to get carried away and use it too frequently. When both hands are brought forward to release the rein simultaneously the horse should slightly lower its head without any loss of tempo, demonstrating its state of balance and confidence in the rider's hands, and that it is not relying on the

Fig 100 Surrendering both reins.

reins for support. This exercise is included in some dressage tests for this reason.

The German name 'Uberstreichen' for these rein actions has been difficult to translate, and has often been referred to as 'stroking the horse's neck', which the uninitiated have taken literally. Perhaps 'surrendering the rein' is the nearest and best interpretation of this useful and informative exercise.

When the outside rein is released on a stiff horse it may help it turn to the inside. If so, ask yourself whether you were holding the horse up on that rein. When you give the inside hand, does the horse turn its head in the opposite direction? If it does, then it is not sufficiently in balance or supple enough to hold its bend while you release the rein momentarily. This implies that it needs to take more notice of your inside leg in that particular direction.

Another bonus resulting from this rein release procedure is the relaxation which it produces in the horse's mouth, mainly because the rider relaxes his or her arms, releasing undue tension on the rein.

Signals do not operate in isolation. Every movement made between the horse and rider must be interpreted in the context of the whole relationship. The rider's whole body speaks to the horse, not just the limbs relaying the communications in a more obvious way. Every movement is accentuated at the end of the limbs, rather like the arc which a pendulum makes even though its point of origin moves very little. Movement always starts with intention, however subtle this may be. The more aware you can become, the more you will realise that this is indeed the case.

The basic grammar of equestrian language, as accepted in Great Britain and the Continent, is fairly standardised, being based on that used in classical riding traditions such as the Spanish Riding School. This provides a common language between all riders and horses, but it does not follow that variations do not arise. Every rider has his or her own individual interpretation of the basic instructions to the horse. Riders thus need to attune their signals when taking over a strange horse for the first time. Horses too vary in their sensitivity and are vulnerable to changes. It is important to avoid confusing them.

When the time comes for riders to learn how to extend their influence over their horse and increase their repertoire of movements, remembering what to do with this or that hand or leg can produce considerable anxiety. When the other requirements of a good performance are added to the list, such as the way in which the rider should sit and the correct shape of the horse, there is a formidable amount clamouring for the rider's attention. It is often the initial encounter with the complexities involved in riding language which produces the tendency to become too 'end-result orientated'. This is when calmness and relaxation are most needed, for learning their language means keeping an eye on priorities rather than generalities, knowing that when you can communicate with the horse, things begin to fall naturally into their appointed place.

As an example of the signalling code in operation, let us look at the canter transition of the horse. A trained horse will be able to understand the rider's request for a specific leading leg. If the rider decides to ask the horse to strike off on its near fore, the message from the rider will come via the left rein to position the head very slightly towards the leading leg, then the outside rein to support the position. The rider's right (outside) leg will come slightly further back to hold the quarters in position and continue the pace while the left leg is used to ask for the impulsion which creates the transition. A bird's eye view would give an impression of the horse moving very slightly around the rider's left leg.

These references to 'inside' and 'outside' relate to the horse's position on a bend. The horse is said to be on the left rein when going round in an anti-clockwise direction, and to be on right rein when travelling clockwise. In this situation, 'inside' and 'outside' are quite clear. However, once this primary concept of the horse's position is understood it can then be taken into any context, not only in relation to the direction in the school, but with reference to the actual position of the horse's body in any movement, so that what appears to be a contradiction, which arises when a horse is executing counter canter on a circle, suddenly becomes relevant. At this stage, it is the horse's position only to which the terms 'inside' and 'outside' refer, for the horse who is working in a counter canter position, will have his body positioned very slightly like a banana round the rider's outside leg.

This situation can seem illogical on first appearances but when the time arrives for you to perform at this level, the inside and outside of the horse's body and the signals pertinent to its direction will clarify themselves in a practical way. To the natural riding enthusiast this may all sound rather mind-boggling. There is no need to become over-concerned, because when you make one step it leads to the next. When you give your attention to one part of any operation, the others tend to fall into place anyway.

On one occasion, a pupil was having a canter problem with her medium dressage horse. In this particular case, the horse was not changing pace smoothly or quickly enough for the rider. The delay and consequent jerkiness of the transition was, on the contrary, becoming more pronounced. She was asked by the coach what she was trying to do. She replied with a string of instructions which she expected the horse to obey.

'Which one is the most interesting, and how would you like it to feel?' she was asked. She chose to monitor the feeling on the rein as the horse was asked to canter, and she chose the word 'soft' to describe it. Using numbers from one to ten to keep track of any variation while she applied the technique, she soon found that the transitions were transformed. She realised that she had been trying too hard to make too many things happen at once. Now she had rediscovered, through awareness, that when she observed the most important thing all her other troubles disappeared.

The forward impetus and direction of the horse have so far received most of our attention. Now it is time to look at regulating and controlling the speed at which the horse travels.

Controlling the Speed

A young horse does not instinctively respond to the hand signals of the rider, which means that it has to be taught what they mean before it will yield to the feeling on the rein instead of resisting it. If this habit of resistance persists, it can easily turn into a tug of war with the

Fig 101   Rider and horse pulling at one another.

rider. The mouth of the horse is also open to abuse, being such a sensitive part of its anatomy. Sensitive hands are some fortunate riders' prerogative, but they need not be an exclusive gift; they can be developed through increased awareness. One of the ball games can help, because it amplifies the sensation of varying tension which the rider can learn to recognise. This results in both horse and rider having the confidence to hold the rein comfortably between them. When this happens it is known as having a good contact with one another.

When one partner increases the tension, resistance will take place. The horse will set its jaw against the rider's hand in protest, and the rider will match it with more pulling. Because the horse is so much stronger, this confrontation can

only end in the horse's favour.

Non-resistance is more likely to be successful, since a horse cannot pull against itself. Having the confidence to let go even slightly takes some courage in certain situations, but with experience the result of this giving and taking on the rein will prove its effectiveness.

THE HALT

When the rider wants to slow down or stop, the outside rein is the one with which the message is given, while the inside rein keeps the horse's direction. All hand signals require back-up from the rider's legs. This results in the horse's energy being pushed back into the rider's hands, keeping the horse in a state of balance, so that obedience becomes a physical possibility. The further the horse can bring its hind legs underneath its body, the lighter it becomes in front, and stopping or slowing down does not result in a wheelbarrow effect which makes it so difficult for the horse to stop. Once the horse is leaning on the reins for support this cannot happen even if it wants it to.

Instructions to riders to squeeze the rein to produce deceleration can often be misinterpreted, but the ball exercise soon produces the desired results. An interesting phenomenon emerges when riders take hold of the rein in an assortment of unnatural attitudes. Somehow, the thin hard material produces an awkwardness, but it disappears entirely when the riders are asked to hold the balls, or to change them over. The reins themselves seem to create an artificiality in the use of the hand which is not seen in any other circumstances. When a ball is about to be changed to the opposite hand, both hands will naturally be at the correct level and in the correct position for holding the reins. This is seen in the unbroken line formed by the rein running directly from the horse's mouth to the rider's elbow. It is the elbow which is the joint which forms the hinge, providing the elasticity with which the rider can follow the nodding of the horse's head, thus letting the hand become part of the overall movement. Riders should think in terms of giving their hands to the horse. Once the ball exercise has provided the feeling of softness which can exist between the hands and the horse's mouth, the rider is much more likely to be able to relax and let it happen.

As we have seen, intention on its own is often sufficient to send a message to the horse, and can be useful in alerting it to any change of plan. For instance, when slowing down or stopping, it is often the rider's own body which actually slows down and warns the horse. Should the rider be doing rising trot when he or she decides to slow down, they should ease up on their movement before sitting down in the saddle to give the actual message. This is done by closing both legs to keep the horse in balance, and keeping its direction with the help of the inside rein. The slowing down action then takes place on the outside rein through a series of intermittent squeezes. By giving the horse time to organise itself for changes of pace and direction, it will remain calm and relaxed. Remember that horses have one-track minds, and respond readily to a clear message. Each message needs accurate timing in relation to the horse's responses, and it is important to avoid giving when the horse takes and taking when the horse gives. The ability to do the opposite, to give when the horse gives and take when the horse takes, is the hallmark of an educated rider.

The way in which a horse comes to a halt indicates the depth or deficiency of its training. The way the rider halts also tells the same story, as well as showing how they feel during the process, especially if any duress arises, such as the horse deciding to ignore the given signals. This situation can arise in a dressage competition when the rider is trying to do his or her best and has to produce a halt as part of the first movement. Undue haste or apprehension at this point in the competition can cause resentment in the horse, which shows in the raising of its head, the opening of its mouth, a general stiffening of its body from head to tail, with maybe even a swish of its tail as it

Fig 102 The halt.

demonstrates its irritability. Once the rider resorts to forcing the issue, the halt becomes associated in the horse's mind with discomfort. If, on the other hand, the horse can experience that the result of being co-operative is freedom from restriction, it will be more willing to carry out its rider's wishes.

How you execute the halt is more important to begin with than where you halt. To take the strain out of teaching your horse to stop, you can use a targeting exercise which combines the 'how' and the 'where' without imposing too much pressure on the horse. Choose a place where you want to change pace from trot to walk, and mark the exact

spot in some way. This is a visualisation exercise, so you want to feel very relaxed while you run through an imaginary sequence of coming up to your marker and changing pace smoothly and softly. Think of as many details as possible, such as the horse's head, neck, ears and overall shape and depth. Think about the speed and how you want it to feel as you execute the transition. Then put it into practice without any physical effort and notice what happens. That, apart from keeping the picture of doing it firmly in your mind's eye, is all you have to do. What happened? The chances are that the horse hesitated even if it did not change pace. Practise this a few times and let the horse respond in its own way, then begin to put it into practice for your halting. Remember that the horse needs a time lapse of three or four steps to bring itself forward into balanced immobility, so do allow for this.

Another awareness exercise for halting is to count the number of steps it takes for the horse to come to a standstill while you quietly give and take on the rein. Your awareness of the steps taken will reduce the tendency to pressure the horse into halting, and will keep you relaxed, so that you do not intervene at that moment. Repeat this as often as you like, rewarding the horse generously whenever it stops. You can then take this a step further by judging the distance you are from your target, accepting any obedience with gratitude. The reasons for evaluating any discrepancy in exact measurement are two-fold. First, it provides facts: 'I am one and a half metres (five feet) beyond the target', rather than fantasy: 'That was a bad attempt'. Secondly, it will allow adjustments to take place in your body almost without your knowing, but which the horse will readily recognise. This will happen only when you and your horse remain attentive and relaxed.

THE REIN BACK

When the horse has learnt to come to a halt with relaxed obedience, then teaching him to rein back will have fewer problems. This is a useful extension of the horse's repertoire as, for example, when opening or closing a gate.

Once the horse understands that it moves forward into the rein contact when it is asked to halt, the signal to rein back becomes a logical progression. The only difference in the signal is the increased pressure on the rein which, as it were, dominates the combined effect of the rider's legs and hands, and which persuades the horse to step back. When this happens it should be rewarded instantly, and the request reward sequence used intermittently, as the horse begins to understand.

The diagonal sequence of legs which are seen when the horse reins back correctly will develop if its early lessons foster calmness, roundness and relaxation. When force is resorted to or too many steps are expected, the horse's resistance can not only block the way to success but unpleasant associations will affect other attempts. Once the horse raises its head and hollows its back it is virtually impossible for the horse to obey. This manoeuvre increases the pressure on the horse's back so it is important to 'think' of sitting lightly on the saddle so that it can move back without inhibition. When this happens easily, the rein back becomes another routine which further increases the carrying capacity and power of its quarters.

There is no reason why the rein back cannot be introduced as a dismounted exercise by gently tapping each foreleg in turn with the whip while saying 'back', but remember to be satisfied with one or two steps at first and do not ask for more than three or four even when the horse has become proficient. After all, free forward movement is still the intention of the horse's activity. When its paces are even and flowing and changes of direction and circles can be performed with suppleness, the transitions which link them together become smooth and spontaneous. The halts will begin to take place without resistance, because the horse's

Fig 103 Incorrect way to rein back.

Fig 104 Correct way to rein back.

mental and physical attitude will make it possible to carry out the rider's wishes in an alert and co-operative way. The rider's signals, produced by the thoughts which instigated them, will gradually become more subtle as the mental attitude between horse and rider becomes close.

As Colonel Llewelyn says in his foreword to Lucy Rees' book *The Horse's Mind*: 'I have recorded elsewhere how Foxhunter, my showjumper, who clearly loved showjumping, could read my mind as I could read his. If I wanted him to stop I hardly had to do anything. He just knew what I was thinking.' When you reach this point, the signalling code has gone through the cycle from simplicity to complexity, and returned full circle to a refined simplicity which is only possible when total understanding and trust exists between horse and rider.

9 Connections

In this chapter the pieces of the jigsaw are put together to make a more complete picture of the horse and rider's progress.

With regard to the horse, the official dressage rule book describes the attributes which good training produces. These are:

- freedom and regularity of paces;
- harmony, lightness and ease of movement;
- the lightness of the forehand and engagement of the quarters, originating in lively impulsion;
- the acceptance of the bridle with submissiveness throughout and without tenseness or resistance.

Reading this list of qualities in the dressage horse, and remembering that the word 'dressage' means 'training', you might feel like adding or subtracting some descriptive words of your own. Words are evocative, they create feelings or memories. They are also emotive, exciting and arouse the feelings and, if used positively, they can be very effective training tools. The more you become aware of this, the more helpful and imaginative words will spring to mind.

Writing down the qualities of good training in your own words is both a creative exercise and perhaps a revealing one as well. It will activate both hemispheres of your brain, giving the intuitive right side a chance to speak more clearly to you.

The advantages of a sound training for both horse and rider are obvious, and the horse, just like a child, is always happier when it has experienced the security of logical discipline which gives it safe boundaries and makes it feel more comfortable with humans and with equine companions.

As you work together with more information and experience at your disposal, the process of your horse's development can be likened to an old car which, to begin with, leaves much to be desired in springing, steering and braking systems. The transformation which comes about with patient training can turn it into a limousine or sports car, with superior suspension, press-button control and synchromesh gears.

One danger is, however, that while enjoying these results it is easy to forget where you started from. It helps to recall this from time to time, to keep your progress in perspective and to avoid making false assumptions about how quickly you should proceed.

The proof of the transformation is seen when it becomes possible to ride an impromptu sequence of exercises at all paces, and as dictated by your coach or a friend. This means that you get very little

warning of the next manoeuvre, and it requires maximum control and accuracy. It also demonstrates the effective ratio of time, weight, space and flow in your movements. Such an exercise means you have to let 'Self 2', your automatic pilot, come to the fore, as 'Self 1' listens to the directions. Letting your body do what it hears in this intuitive way will give you the feeling of mental balance and relaxation.

You can do a similar exercise on your own, riding movements which seem to suggest themselves through your horse. Try imagining them as a pattern of different colours, like a tapestry which is framed by your arena or field boundaries. Another way of putting your exercises together is to visualise the activity as a dance, with different steps and tempos, the theme of which is the smoothness with which all the variations are executed.

To reach this stage, both you and your horse will need to practise exercises to make you more supple. You will also need to expand your awareness of the way these activities will influence your own body. Once your horse is willing to obey your legs when you ask for forward impulsion and accept the contact of the reins quietly, steering will become much easier.

The energy which the horse produces from its hind legs, which you might think of as an outboard motor, actually begins to feel more like an inboard motor as the hind legs come forward further under the body. This makes it easier for the horse to find its balance while changing direction, performing circles and going round corners.

The next step is to ask the horse to become more aware of the rein contact, and to increase its confidence in it by flexing at the poll and in the lower jaw whenever the rider asks the horse to step up with its hind legs. This should be done without letting the horse increase the pace. This combination of the rider's legs and hands slightly increases the pressure on the horse's mouth unless it yields in the way described. When the horse does this, it is said to be 'on the bit'. This results in an overall change of shape in its body as it shortens it slightly by becoming more round and brings its head into an almost vertical position. In accepting this situation, the horse relaxes its back and puts itself in a state of alert purpose, at the disposal of its rider.

The rider's responsibility is to bring the horse to this stage of development, and then to implement this new request with sensitivity. This is not always easy if the horse's previous experience has been a painful one, so it is helpful to look at some of the problems which arise in relation to a horse's mouth.

Improved Rein Contact

The horse's acceptance of the rider's hand on the reins has a major influence on its overall deportment. This can change dramatically if it is frightened by the pain in its mouth. It is no mean thing to ask a horse to tolerate the variety of metal bits in its mouth which provide the rider with the necessary control. That bits should be humane goes without saying, for the barbarity of some past inventions is beyond belief. Many of the old Victorian bits produced sufficient leverage to break

Fig 105   On the bit.

Fig 106   Overbent.

Fig 107   Above the bit.

145

a horse's jaw, and it is a merciful improvement that the snaffle is now in much more general use. Even the snaffle bit, however, can inflict pain if it is fitted badly or used in the wrong hands. Combined with a tight drop noseband, it can inflict considerable pain and restriction, often in a less obvious way.

A horse must gain confidence in its rider's ability to keep a steady tension on the reins, which is known as 'keeping the contact'. If the horse's head has become unsteady as a result of some unhappy experience in the past, it may prove difficult to introduce a consistent and reliable tension on the rein, and thus to prevent a constant jerking of its bit, as it throws its head about to avoid it.

When this happens, the horse becomes very tense, and this can make the rider tense too as a result of the effort of trying to find some stability for the hands. The solution is to follow the horse with the hands wherever its head goes, rather like keeping a fish on a line while you bring it ashore, where a slack line can mean a broken one and a lost fish with a hook in its mouth. When the horse drops the tension on the rein, this produces a sudden jerk when contact is made again. This creates a very unsatisfactory relationship between the horse and rider as both compete to see who will let go first.

Trying to ride with a very light rein is not necessarily the answer, as it often proves difficult to maintain. The horse can sense this and feel insecure in the rider's hands. It is much better to take a firmer hold on the reins to give the horse confidence, just as you would take a child by the hand to cross a road. The key to maintaining good contact is to find out what tension on the rein is acceptable to both horse and rider.

When you have established a confident and reliable contact you will notice a change both in your deportment as a rider and in the shape of your horse. The mutual comfort you achieve will allow the rider to become taller while sitting closer in the saddle, and the horse to become rounder in outline, once it stops evading the bit. This permits the horse to lower its head and neck to seek the contact on the reins, thus freeing its back which comes up into a strong flexible position as the hind legs engage under the body. When this happens, the horse develops the ability to carry itself better, because it can now move its centre of gravity back off its shoulders to behind the withers. The more the hind legs engage, the better able they are to take their share of weight, rather than keeping the weight on the forehand which can easily become overloaded in early training.

Improved Carriage

Improved balance in the horse precedes improved carriage, a step further in a horse's development and related to the carrying capacity of its hind legs. As the rider takes up a more elegant attitude, balance and carriage combine to create a pleasing poise. In natural riding classes these two developments have sometimes coincided spontaneously, to the surprise of all involved.

Improved carriage implies that the horse has not only lowered its head and neck as it has relaxed, but has gone a stage further, showing confidence in the rein contact by relaxing its lower jaw. This alters the angle of the head until it is just in front of the perpendicular. When the horse does this, the rider will notice the softer, lighter feeling on the reins, and a sense of the horse being totally at his or her disposal as it continues to maintain its forward movement.

This technique is much desired, and it is hardly surprising that it is sometimes forced on a horse when the rider is in a hurry and wants the horse to look correct. When results are brought about in this way, it will tend to produce a backlash of tension in both horse and rider.

Putting too much emphasis on achieving good carriage before the rider and horse are adequately prepared can result in riders developing a complex about it. There is no need to be obsessively anxious about the horse 'being on the bit' because, working with the awareness concept, you can produce it without too much effort as a natural consequence of your natural riding routines. When good carriage is achieved, it is a very positive step forward and indicates how much confidence the rider and horse have in one another.

An unusual example of the progression from balance to carriage happened in a beginner's lesson. Bob was an Inner Game coach with very little experience of riding, and what riding he had done was in Australia without instruction. He borrowed a horse for his lesson, which proved to be a very fit hunter, the size of which he found daunting. As the horse was rather fresh, the coach asked the owner to settle it down before Bob mounted. This gave Bob time to observe how the horse was ridden, and the coach a chance to assess its suitability. The horse in question had a very high head carriage, and as a result moved with a very hollow back and was very tense. When Bob

mounted, he spent some time finding his balance by exploring various lengths for his stirrups. Finally he was ready to be led round the school. Now he took time to experience the walking sensation and some basic controls, which involved turning the horse and stopping it. He was soon walking about the school solo and, as he gained more confidence, began to talk about trotting.

The coach kept asking him about his balance and what he noticed, and decided to let him trot the next time he asked, the horse by now being marvellously co-operative. When the horse moved into a trot it became clear that Bob was rising in a very laboured way, so attention was turned to this. The coach asked Bob which was the more noticeable, the up movement or the down movement. Bob's immediate answer was 'the down beat' but he then also realised the up beat was too high and took too long, with the result that he lost his balance and fell back into the saddle. This brought the topic of rhythm to the fore. The coach now decided to use the Inner Game of tennis technique of 'bounce/hit' instead of concentrating on the 'up/down'. By moving Bob's attention to 'bounce/hit' rhythm, the exercise eliminated the faulty 'up' of Bob's rise. The outcome was successful and, finding himself in time with the horse, Bob began to move the horse more easily round the school.

Suddenly the horse dropped its head, became round, and relaxed its body, so that it was actually working on the bit. No one was more surprised than the coach. By this time Bob was tired, so it was decided to give the owner a short lesson in return for having lent Bob her horse.

When the owner mounted, she was

asked what she would like to do. She immediately said, 'I've been trying for so long to get my horse's head down, without success. Perhaps now Bob has managed it I could do it too.'

There was really only one significant difference between the two riders, but the horse recognised it immediately. One rider was relaxed and not trying, while the other was desperate to make her horse go in a certain way. As we have seen, a useful tool to facilitate any progressive step is to visualise it taking place. For example, if you have seen a horse ridden on the bit, you will have a good idea of the picture it presents. This mental exercise can really work for you and accelerate your progress without riding. As Dr Harry Emerson Fosdick says in Dr Maltz's book *Psycho Cybernetics:*

Hold a picture of yourself long enough in your mind's eye and you will be drawn towards it. Picture yourself vividly as defeated and that alone will make victory impossible. Picture yourself vividly as winning and that alone will contribute immeasurably to success.

With practice, it is possible to flash this positive imagery on and off your mental screen at will, and this will help your body to conform to it. Seeing yourself riding your horse in the way you desire helps it to happen. The shape of both your own body and that of the horse will change. As a rider who was also an artist once remarked:

A good design or shape always works successfully, whether it is a simple inanimate object in daily use or a horse and rider.

It may be difficult to believe that such a simple ploy as visualisation can work, but it will if you practise regularly. When people have been asked to do a visualisation exercise and then put it in operation to describe the way they want to see themselves, their physical portrayal is usually spot on. Positive images have a magnetic quality, so keep them in mind instead of unhelpful negative images. This diversion will help you and the horse to feel relaxed as you approach the more complex aspects of riding.

Another good mental exercise is to choose evocative words to describe sensations or appearances. These again need to be positive, and should become a part of your mental vocabulary. They can work via your subconscious mind, so that you can summon them up almost magically. Using the word 'airborne' for your canter, for example, can be very inspirational. Some pupils prefer to use colours to describe their feelings or the different paces of their horse, and they will sometimes use them instead of the numbers game. A pupil might use different colours for the rising and sitting trot, or even shades of the same colour. A comfortable sitting trot sensation might be deep blue, and recalling this colour and concentrating on it can help to recapture the sensation without the danger of trying too hard. The same process happens with the evocative words which programme your self-conscious mind. You can use them in times of crisis as well as moments of pleasure and in doing so you will remain in a more relaxed and receptive state.

Improved Transitions

When the horse and rider have become more familiar with their increasing athletic ability, the overall standard of performance can be evaluated. This will include scrutiny of the transitions linking the paces with one another.

When transitions take place smoothly, with the horse remaining on the bit and without loss of tempo in the preceding pace, the rider will realise the importance of relaxation. The use of evocative words can help to record this feeling of relaxation when it arises. Your horse will begin to relax too, and its increased co-operation and acceptance will become evident in the way it is able to change from one pace to the other, change directions and perform circles, loops and transitions with smoothness and balance.

Transitions are significant moments of truth in relation to the horse's balance and suppleness, and it is during their execution that resistance sometimes becomes evident. It is therefore important to understand why resistance arises and to be able to avoid it by not making excessive demands on the horse.

There are two stages of development in the horse's ability to change pace smoothly: progressive transition and direct transition.

With a young horse that lacks balance, changes of pace must be made progressively. This means the horse only moves up one pace or down one pace, rather like the notes of a musical scale. This is called progressive transition, the calm and slow practice of which eventually increases the horse's ability to balance itself.

At a later stage, the horse will be able to miss out the connecting pace and go, for example, from trot to halt or walk to canter without becoming tense. These are called direct transitions, some of which are more difficult than others, as an alert rider will soon discover. Trot to halt is generally a more difficult transition than walk to canter, though generalities are misleading as the degree of difficulty will vary from horse to horse.

Riders are often surprised at the ease with which their horses are able to do this at a certain point in their training. When riders are asked to try it for the first time, they often react by looking surprised and saying, 'Goodness, is that really possible?' Their horses frequently give them a surprisingly positive response.

Transitions also have another bonus, for they help to keep the horse alert. This, combined with the physical usefulness of transitions, makes them a vital link in the overall performance. They hold the jigsaw together.

Transitions are not confined to changes of pace because changes can be made within each pace. For instance, the trot can be accelerated or decelerated. Working trot, for example, which is the one normally used at novice level, can become medium trot and extended trot, both of which demand an increasing length of stride and propulsion. Collected trot is at the other end of the scale, a shortened but elevated version of the stride. Similar variations are possible in walk and canter.

Before leaving the subject of pace transitions, it is worth stressing the usefulness of these exercises in the early stages of training the horse to canter. The canter can improve dramatically when regular transitions are introduced rather than trying to keep the horse in canter for too long. A horse which is already on its forehand will become heavy as it tires,

Fig 108 Medium trot.

Fig 109 Extended trot.

150

Fig 110   Collected trot.

and forcing it to keep going in this way can only be detrimental. The rider who listens carefully will notice when there is any change in the regularity of the horse's footfall and will recognise that it signifies a loss of balance.

Any variation in or change of pace involves the adjustment of the horse's centre of gravity. The increasing strength and suppleness of its quarters and hind legs help to move the centre of gravity back, freeing the horse's shoulders. This makes all the difference to the ease and rapidity with which the horse can change from one pace to another, or change direction.

How all this can be achieved can become very technical and demanding, particularly for the horse, so it is important to stay in the present and concentrate on one thing at a time. The emphasis on doing one thing at a time is most important when it comes to competition per-formance, where there is more pressure than ever to think about too many things all at once. Remind yourself that when you stay in the present there is all the time you need. Trust 'Self 2' with time – it has a wonderful in-built mechanism which knows how to use time to its best advan-tage. If events happen slowly now, this can be made up at a later stage. Pupils who do not worry about time tend to overtake those who fight it.

The Importance of Rest

Rest is something else we do not utilise to its fullest extent. Remember how latent learning can happen between lessons, and how the subconscious mind continues to work while the body is at rest. Muscles are developed more effectively if exertion is preceded by a restful pause. If you raise your arms and pause before and after each movement, for example, this allows the blood supply to replenish itself and to remove waste products. Muscles which accumulate lactic acid through fatigue will cease to function efficiently.

In relation to the horse, adequate rest also means not persisting too long with any activity. You may well ask how long is too long, and the answer is that your heightened awareness will provide the clues. First the horse may feel less lively, for example, or may start to resist. If so, stop and watch the horse's breathing. This may be hurried, making the nostrils dilate and the flanks heave. Accelerated respiration can have other causes, but it often results from the horse holding its breath, just as you, the rider, do when you are tense. An unfit horse is more likely to be put under pressure in this way, because it has little stamina with which to make the effort required.

Riding on a Long Rein

This is a valuable part of the exercise routine, since it offers the reward of reduced effort. There are two distinct stages: riding on a loose rein without any contact, and riding on a long rein while contact is maintained. In both instances, the horse should lower its head and stretch its neck fully when given the opportunity to do so. This obviously rests the front part of the horse, but this position will also stretch the back muscles causing the back to come up under the rider as the hind legs step further underneath. Try bending your whip into a 'U' shape, then reverse it so the 'U' is upside-down. This will show you what happens to the horse's back as it is allowed to stretch its spine. It is therefore possible to rest the horse and at the same time provide a useful therapy for its back muscles.

With practice, long-rein or loose-rein riding can be done at all paces. The rider must make sure that his or her body language is clear, since pulling the hands back along the reins towards the abdomen before releasing them contradicts the desired intention, and the horse knows this. Instead, put your hands forward slowly and open your fingers, saying to the horse, 'Here are the reins, take them and stretch.' If you have been riding forward freely your horse will comply. If not, you will have to review what you have been doing with your hands. A horse unwilling to take the opportunity of respite has been restricted in some way, and you will need to regain its understanding and trust. Fig 111 expresses the horse's freedom in the new contact.

The value of riding on a loose or long rein is lost if the rider switches off and 'abandons the ship', which often happens. This is not the time for the rider to take a rest. The rider's role is to help the horse make the most of the opportunity by slackening his or her hands, lightening the weight in the saddle and monitoring the speed which the horse finds most comfortable. The horse must balance itself as it adjusts to these changes, and the rider needs to register any new sensations which take place.

Directing the horse in this situation has lessons for the rider as well as for the horse. It will require the support of the rider's inside leg, and perhaps the whip lying on the horse's shoulder to begin with in order to keep it in the track when riding round the arena. Horses soon learn to do this and to maintain a steady speed which eliminates any sense of rushing or loss of control.

Fig 111   A long rein.

A horse whose mouth has been abused in the past will be most reluctant to stretch, and will rely on the rider to guide and show it what to do until it understands that it has permission to take the rein without being punished by a jab in the mouth for doing so. If the horse is reluctant, remember to praise any tentative gestures it may make. If the horse has been held back by the rider's hands or too severely bitted it is hardly surprising that it lacks confidence. These symptoms show that the horse has not experienced what is meant by free forward movement, which should be one of the first priorities in its training.

Any schooling session should begin by giving the horse five minutes on a long rein, and at least one similar interlude during the work. When a lesson has been completed, another five minutes should be allowed for the horse to stretch its body as a final reward and relaxation. This provides fertile soil for latent learning, the learning which is going on whether you are actually riding or not.

Rewarding your Horse

Rest is a reward which horses soon learn to appreciate. Talking of rewards, have you thought of the variety of ways in which you can say thank you to your horse or give it encouragement when it shows a glimmer of understanding? The ways in which you can say thank you vary in their degree of impact, and can be used appropriately as results justify them. They include:

- patting;
- stopping a signal;
- stopping the lesson;
- speaking to the horse;
- changing to a different exercise;
- taking the horse out of the school for a ride;
- putting the horse in the field;
- putting the horse in the stable;
- giving the horse a tit-bit;
- providing a static rest interlude during the ride;
- dismounting while this takes place, especially with a young horse;
- surrendering the reins;
- dismounting at the end of a lesson and leading the horse back to the stable;
- riding on a long or loose rein.

You could try putting these in order of merit to see how you judge their relative importance. Think about what your horse has to do to earn the reward of its lesson being over for the day. How much does the time available govern your decision?

One rider provided her own answer when she had been working hard with an exercise to help the horse to balance on a circle. Carried away by trying to get results, rather than monitoring the process itself, she had been very active with her inside leg. She began to complain that her leg was aching. Suddenly she realised that if her leg was aching, the horse's legs might also be feeling fatigued, and that it was trying too hard that had produced this result. It had come about through worrying that time was running out, and

the desperation to achieve a result before the bell went took over her sense of priorities. The recognition of what had happened did, however, help to find an appropriate reward for the horse when it was most needed.

Balancing in Turns and Circles

The difficulty described above, which horses often encounter when finding their balance in turns and circles, is usually due to shortage of training, or perhaps no training at all. Helping your horse to become laterally supple can start in the stable. It will make you more aware of your horse's limitations before you try to do something about it when you are mounted.

Try bending your horse's neck gently one way and then the other. While you do this, notice whether it resents this in any way, and also if the muscles on one side of the neck are more developed. Notice how far the neck can bend without the horse moving a foreleg, and compare the degree of bend in each direction to see if there is any difference. Find out if your horse's neck is tender when you press it. How does it show that it hurts? It is surprising how horses can put their messages across if you are sensitive to their reactions.

Residual tension in a horse's neck when at rest will not go away when you ride. Sometimes this condition can be aggravated by memories of painful injections or being ridden in running reins. Massaging the muscles which feel hard to the touch can start the therapeutic process and bring the feeling back into this area.

The horse's back can also cause difficulties when it is asked to circle. The spine is naturally rigid, and it is thought that the muscles which slightly displace the rib-cage give the illusion of the horse bending uniformly throughout its length. The horse appears to be flatter on the inside and fuller on the outside when it is performing this movement correctly.

If the back muscles involved are too underdeveloped or overworked there is bound to be a reaction, so it is important to check the horse's back regularly after the introduction of new exercises for signs of tenderness, which can occur more often and more quickly than is realised. When this situation arises, the horse is not only physically inhibited but mentally distracted as well.

If the shoulder falls in whenever you turn your horse, it is impossible to position the head in the direction of movement. This means that the rider will need to use the inside leg to ask the horse to move away from it in order to recover its balance. When the horse understands this signal, its response will cause a slight sideways shift of weight as it moves away from the thrust of its inside leg, which is now placed underneath the body for support.

This gentle easing over is called leg yielding (*see* page 129), and is usually performed while moving from the outer track of the school onto the inner one. Initially, however, a horse will get the message more easily when it is asked to move from the inner track to the outer one, because the horse's inclinination is to move outward. Riders who do not have schooling facilities can use a quiet lane for this exercise. Once you can move your horse in this oblique direction, it will be much easier to deal with problems of balance whenever you are turning.

If you start with a twenty-metre (sixty-five foot) circle and gradually decrease it in size, this will increase the bend in the horse's body. You can then start to increase the circle again, pushing the horse outwards to the original circle in response to your inside leg.

Technically this is no longer called leg yielding, because the horse is working in a bend to make the circle. 'Leg yielding' is really moving from one straight line to another line parallel with the first, the horse's head being flexed only slightly away from its direction of travel.

These are basic exercises which enable the horse to remain vertical in its turns and circles, and not capsize like a ship in rough weather. With increasing lateral suppleness, combined with the improvement in longitudinal suppleness which comes from the practice of transitions, the horse gradually becomes more pliant in changes of pace and direction. This quality naturally brings greater accuracy into all its work, as well as improving the bounce and buoyancy of the paces themselves.

RELAXING – HORSE AND RIDER

Relaxation is all-important in any new work. If the horse is relaxed it will be softer and more likely to give what little flexibility it has. If you tighten the horse up with too much effort, you will only make it shorter. Being shorter, the horse will naturally become stiffer. To counter this, the horse needs the space that a longer rein will give it, and as it makes use of the long rein in stretching, it has more chance of being able to bend. By working slowly in walk you will be able to find out for yourself what your horse is able to do and where you think you ought to put your attention. You may find the game where you hold balls in your hands is useful for this. Try carrying one ball in either hand on both reins, or a ball in each hand may work better for you. Because no two people are the same, it is important that you use these experimental exercises in your own individual way. When you do this you will be able to find out what disturbs the balance the most, since if you are not straight in the saddle the horse will have a double problem.

Another important area for your attention is the way your inside leg feels. When you use it, what happens? Do you contract your body and sit over on to the opposite side, or drop your inside shoulder?

When you make new discoveries, choose your own words to describe them, using numbers or colours if this helps you. For instance, you might have a black sensation if your hand feels heavy. Another useful technique is to change any negative words which come to your mind to opposite positive ones.

Circles and loops can stimulate your imagination symbolically. Think what else they might represent – a garden perhaps, a pool, a crater, a wood, or an oasis? As you ride round, fill in the details. Does the bank of the crater seem to crumble away? Does the wind blow you onto the garden when your horse loses its balance? Is there an ogre which pushes your horse beyond the circle's circumference as you pass a certain point on the circle? These images can be allowed to occupy your trying-too-hard 'Self 1', leaving 'Self 2', which actually initiates physical adjustments, to go to work without you actually realising what is happening.

I had an interesting experience of this in my first Inner Game golf lesson. Never having played golf before, my shots were very unpredictable and when I did hit them they lacked any drive. More often I never hit the ball at all. The coach suggested that I might send a message with the next ball as I went to hit it. This I did, and much to my surprise the ball disappeared into the far distance with a resounding clink. 'What did you send with that ball?' he asked in surprise. In fact, I had simply thought the word 'light'. It was a most extraordinary feeling, because there was no obvious effort by my body at all. What had happened was that the magic word allowed my innate physical co-ordination to make the connection. When I tried intellectualising the shot and was trying hard to repeat it, I was completely unsuccessful.

As Dr James Greene writes in Dr Maxwell Maltz's book *Psycho Cybernetics*, 'In many cases the mere relaxation of effort, or too much conscious straining, is in itself enough to eradicate a negative pattern.' Mattias Alexander puts it another way: 'If you stop doing the wrong thing, the right thing can happen.'

All of this adds up to considerable evidence that attentive relaxation is the real 'open sesame'. Even so, attentive relaxation is easier described than done, and reprogramming ourselves after years of conditioning to exert ourselves and try harder means abandoning many of our old concepts.

Once you start to make such a breakthrough you will begin to realise how often we stand in the way of our own progress. We often hang on to a poor self-image which lies about who we really are and what we can do. For instance, if you fail to gain a response from your horse and call yourself a bad rider, this is simply not true. The truth is that you are having difficulties for particular reasons, and you can choose to find out what those reasons are rather than condemning yourself. When you feel you should be doing better, this frequently comes from judging yourself in relation to others, or it may be an excuse like the 'buts' and 'if onlys' of wishful thinking. These expectations refer to a future which is not relevant to the present and indicate a diversion of attention away from the present. They may also suggest hidden goals.

The answer is to clarify these goals and to take stock of what is actually happening in the present. A question worth asking yourself at this point is 'What do I want to do at this moment?' Remember that 'wanting' takes you half-way to your target, whereas 'wishing' means you never start.

By defining intermediate targets, each step on the path becomes more readily accessible and you will begin to gain a sense of purpose. As one thing leads to another, the attention you bring to bear on each step will provide an interesting collection of facts. Those facts will vary in relation to each individual rider, who is pursuing his or her own line of investigation. It becomes quite clear that people do not see, do or appreciate experience in the same ways, just as every horse is different.

Riding a Straight Line

The horse's exercise programme has now come to the point where riding in a straight line has to be considered. In a dressage test this is often the movement which loses marks, as it is both the opening movement and the final one. Pre-competition nerves will show up in the entry of horse and rider, while at the end of the test they are often trying too hard to make the final impression a good one. Of the two, the final straight line ridden down the centre of the arena will usually be the better one.

Riding a straight line challenges the skill of horse and rider. It can easily seem like a tightrope down which they must precariously proceed, and this is often exactly what it looks like to the judge.

It is easier to ride straight lines without wandering from side to side once the circles have improved their shape, because the thing that most helps accuracy is the free forward movement which this exercise develops.

By braving the challenge of riding a straight line with panache and purpose, the likelihood of error is lessened. The ability to ride a direct line with undeflected purpose gives a splendid sense of power if you have the audacity to do it. Once again, games can be helpful. Try thinking about the line symbolically. You could take an urgent message with you for an imaginary recipient. Or you could see how many details you can pick out at the end of your line: 'How many cars are there behind the judge's car?' for example, is a question which sometimes helps competitors.

One thing that is certain is that any unwanted tension will be sure to set off the wandering tendencies, and trying too hard to correct them will only make things worse. When this happens, it is best to keep riding forward with bravado, whatever line you may be on, and even in competitions these tactics will lose less marks than trying to get back to the line. In this situation, the straightening of your horse should not be done by using the leg signals, but with the hands. These should be used to position the horse's forehand in front of its quarters to put it back in its tracks.

The same technique should also be used for halting should the horse step sideways with its hindquarters, making it stand crooked. When the rider pushes the quarters into position with his or her legs, it can result in the horse overdoing the movement at the least provocation, and in so doing finding an easy way of escaping the rider's wishes.

Riding a straight line always involves two turns. The first one puts the horse on course and the second one leads it away, in the opposite direction if a change of rein is intended. Turns are really only corners and it helps to think of them as such, the track made by the horse being seen as a

quarter of a ten- or fifteen-metre (eleven- or sixteen-yard) circle. The execution of a good turn is facilitated for the horse if the rider allows it the length of its body (or more if the horse is stiff) in which to turn. This will mean starting in plenty of time, arriving on the straight line a length from its commencement. Trying to turn an actual right angle with a horse is literally impossible. The horse must be able to accommodate its length in the track it is intended to take. If this is done, the forward impetus will not be impeded by trying to make the horse take a tighter arc, and so it will come round more smoothly with its balance intact. You have to remember that the horse's spine is fairly rigid, with little, if any, movement behind the rib-cage. This leaves the neck as the pliable part of its anatomy, and the neck must not be allowed to bend more than the horse can manage in the rest of its

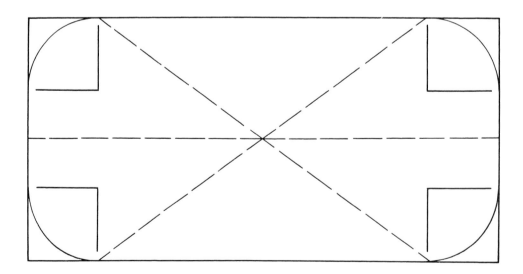

Fig 112   Quadrant on corners and changes of rein.

Fig 113   Use of poles on centre line.

Fig 114   Notice how unlevel stirrups affect the rider's and the horse's balance.

body. This explains why the development of suppleness is not always easy for a horse.

For practice sessions, the sensation of riding on a straight line can be gained with the help of a short line of poles set out like tramlines on the centre line, just after the turn that brings the horse on to it. This gives the horse a straight start, which it may well be able to maintain all the way to the next corner. Fig 113 shows the sense of direction which horse and rider gain from the poles.

This first turn is usually the easiest for the horse, while the second, which takes it in the opposite direction when changing the rein, can be more awkward. Thinking of it from the horse's point of

view, it has to make the first bend to come round, and then straightens its body. Almost as soon as it has done this it must bend again in order to meet the next turn. This amounts to three different positions to be taken up, and if this takes place across the arena instead of down it, there is very little time to spare in the twenty metres (twenty-two yards) available. In fact, it is really less than that, because the horse's track along the side of the school is usually half a metre (two feet) away from the boundary.

Thus, it is little wonder that when the second turn confronts the horse it finds it more difficult, especially when it is being asked to bend in the opposite direction. Should this be on the horse's stiffer side,

159

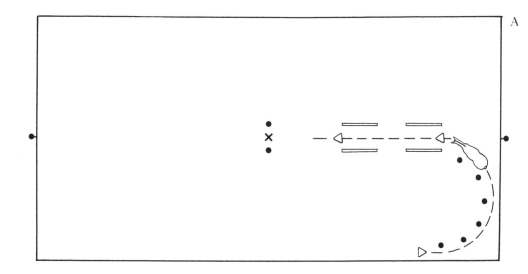

Fig 115   Poles to keep the horse straight.

the difficulty is compounded. While the horse is at this stage of schooling it needs patient preparation for these manoeuvres, while continuing to consolidate its suppling exercises. Gradually the horse will be able to take these changes of rein in its stride without losing the place at either end of the directional route.

Coming to a Halt

The rider's ability to bring the horse to a correct standstill now needs more attention. The obedience being asked of it requires an understanding of the dynamics involved, as the horse needs to engage its revs from its hind legs in order to come to a well-balanced halt. The energy this produces can be directed into the rider's hands through the medium of the reins. These slightly restrict the forward impetus of the horse and contain it so that the horse can, as it were, move its centre of gravity slightly back. This results in a slight lowering of the quarters

The result of this on the horse's energy puts it in a state of lightness on the reins and shoulders, as it contains the power in its hindquarters. The halt brought about by these means has a feeling of forwardness about it, not unlike a car revving for a quick get-away at the traffic lights. In time it will be a natural reaction for the horse to remain on the bit, standing square and immobile, ready to respond to the slightest indication from rider.

The halt can be executed by the fully trained horse from the canter, without the intermediate paces being used. In the earlier training of the horse, however, it is brought about using the progressive transitions which the horse can manage easily.

Fig 116   *Incorrect execution of the halt.*

Fig 117   *Correct execution of the halt.*

Relaxing the Neck and Jaw

We have talked a lot about the horse's development, and the rider's development has moved a little way out of the limelight. It may not be generally realised that the rider too has something to learn in the process of teaching the horse to work on the bit. It may come as a surprise to learn that when our own necks and jaws become tense, it produces a similar contraction of the spine to the one seen in the horse, with the head forced up and backwards. This parallel between horse and rider may be difficult to accept, but anyone who has been taught the Alexander Technique will understand the implications.

Relaxing your neck can begin by placing your fingertips on the muscles which lie on either side of the cervical spine. By moving your head gently backwards and forwards, the tensing and relaxing of these muscles can be felt. An awareness of what the muscles feel like when they are relaxed can imprint the feeling in your mind so that it can be recalled from time to time to help a new habit develop. If you practise enough, this should produce an unconscious response whenever you think of the evocative words you use, such as being 'on the bit' yourself, to recapture a feeling of relaxation.

Relaxing your jaw is helped by letting your lower jaw drop, then breathing out slowly through your mouth until your lungs are empty. Then you can close the jaw. Holding your breath until you feel the need to inhale lets the air come surging effortlessly into the lungs to fill them. Repeat this exercise twice. It has several uses besides being relaxing, for it improves breathing and the use of the voice. It can be done in any spare moments when calmness is needed.

Awareness Exercises

While on the subject of exercises, here are some more which can increase awareness and tone up the body. They are used by Touch for Health enthusiasts, and are said to be beneficial even if they are only practised a few times. They can be done either standing up or lying down, which is even more effective. They have a diagonal movement pattern which is unusual and interesting, and have many permutations limited only by your inventiveness. They improve balance, co-ordination, circulation, stimulate clearer thinking, reduce stress, balance left/right brain activity, relieve stiffness and mobilise the body.

The exercises are a type of exaggerated walking movement, which demonstrate that we often do not move in a true diagonal beat. This may explain why there is an initial sense of awkwardness in executing them and may also highlight why some pupils encounter difficulty in identifying the diagonals of the horse in rising trot. The basic theme is to move the opposite arm and leg simultaneously in the same or opposing directions. Try putting the right arm forward at the same time as the left leg goes forward and keep alternating with the left arm and the right leg in rhythm until you feel the swing of the beat and can keep your balance. Another variation is to move the right arm forward and the left leg back. There are endless variations which can be invented by moving the limbs back, forward, sideways or even across the body or doing twisting movements. Using music can help you to establish a good rhythm. It is also a good idea to note any particular sensation these routines produce.

To underline the importance of the rider's mental attitude which has played such an important part in developing their physical prowess, here is an extract from *Academic Equitation* by General Decarpentry:

The most perfect calmness is essential in a dressage operation. However, despite the finest determination, the rider will not always be able to avoid a shaking of his moral calm and will never be able to recover instantly his physical calm once it has been ruffled, however slight and transient a loss of moral calm.

A flash of temper can inwardly be suppressed almost as soon as it is aroused, but the resulting effect in the rider's nervous tension will persist for some time and, what is more important, for longer than the rider himself realises. The horse on the contrary feels this nervousness and immediately shares it, but needs a much longer time to forget it than the rider. In this respect the horse is gifted with an astonishingly delicate sensitivity, such that even the movements of his ears are a permanent indication of the 'state of the horse's soul' – if this expression can be allowed – which provides the rider with the means of perceiving his own state of nerves, so slight that he may remain unaware of it, and even if his loss of calm is unrelated to the horse's behaviour.

Therefore, as soon as the rider feels any disturbance of his serenity, it is absolutely imperative to allow 'time' for his own physical calm, which determines that of the horse, to be completely restored. A pause, a halt, provided submission is not in question, is necessary before the lesson can continue.

10 Taking Off

Jumping

Jumping serves a valuable purpose for the dressage horse and is an important transitional point of development for both horse and rider. Even for those riders who do not wish to concentrate on jumping, it can be an interesting experience, providing a change of environment and activity which increases the agility of both partners.

Learning to jump is a time for stretching capabilities and extending vistas by going out into the country or on undulating terrain. It is a time to find out what new horizons interest you and what the possibilities are. A launching pad is created by the use of specific gymnastic exercises, designed to encourage greater athletic prowess in the horse.

In one sense, the word 'jumping' is not relevant to this chapter, since any fence under half a metre (two feet) high is not really considered to be a jump. The exercises in this chapter are perhaps better looked upon as change of balance exercises.

THE IMPORTANCE OF CALMNESS

The very word 'jumping' evokes excitement and apprehension, and is a classic example of how strongly words can affect us. Excitement is not the emotion we want to engender, for it can so easily undermine the qualities which training together has already produced. This is why learning to jump can so easily go off the rails. Instead of our patient labours coming to fruition in this activity, we see excitement taking over and casting the benefits already acquired to the four winds.

This becomes particularly obvious when watching a highly-strung and volatile horse impetuously attacking the jumps, showing a clear lack of both mental and physical balance. When this happens the horse's head is usually too high, its mouth is open to resist the bit, and its back is hollow, thus reducing the vital thrust required to clear fences in an easy manner.

This situation happens all too often and is due to ignorance or impatience. It shows a serious breakdown in the relationship between horses and humans. When a horse rushes in to its jumps without waiting for its rider's consent, the comment often made by the rider is, 'My horse loves jumping. I can't stop him.' This is not necessarily the case, since many horses rush in in order to get an unpleasant task over as quickly as possible. It is as if they were shutting their eyes and hoping for the best. There is a hysterical frenzy about these wild-eyed performers which is far removed from the calm and confident picture we have been trying to create.

It is difficult to assess how many riders are prepared to take the time needed for a calm, controlled jumping partnership to emerge. Somehow the temptation to take short cuts and become end-result orientated – in this case, clearing the jumps – becomes too great. The result is that the horse is cheated out of the valuable process of preparation on the ground, before being asked to leave it. When a rider gets carried away so readily, it is easy to see how the horse is affected by this attitude. Excitement often hides an element of fear, and as a result an inexperienced horse can easily lose its confidence. It is important to remember that seventy-five per cent of jumping is actually done on the ground between the fences, and that the jumps themselves actually take very little time to execute.

If ever a word needed engraving on the rider's heart in this activity, it is the word 'calmness'. Calmness holds the key to the continuity of steady logical routines which bring the horse, like the dancer or the gymnast, to a point where flight, however momentary, becomes possible. Anyone willing to practise the ground work calmly, patiently and thoroughly will enjoy taking off with their horse with a confident serenity which allows them both the full use of their potential.

When a course of jumps is negotiated by a competent rider and a confident horse, it has all the components of music. There is the phrasing of pace between each fence, and there is the crescendo of power as each fence is approached without any loss of rhythm in the horse's movement, followed by the climax of the horse thrusting itself into the air. The flight over the fence forms an acrobatic parabola, and, as the horse lands and gathers itself together, the music changes and then repeats its theme. This standard of performance has breath-taking moments, which account for the thrill that makes this such an addictive sport. It is very impressive to watch as horse and rider flow round the jumping circuit as one fluid and accurate entity.

The horse needs to go freely forward, not rushing or hanging back, but confident enough to proceed without hesitation towards and over what the rider confronts it with. It goes without saying that the horse must trust the rider's judgement of what it can and cannot do. As the horse moves forward it faces a new and important challenge when obstacles are placed in its path, but it still needs to move rhythmically in its stride as it approaches them. The horse's round outline has a significant influence on its agility. This shape will have been established in its basic training, as already explained, and, if it can be maintained in the jumping situation, will result in more power in its hind legs in the take-off phase of the jump and give its body the maximum scope when it is in the air. On the other hand, when the desired deportment is lost and the horse's head is raised,

Fig 118   *A bad approach to the jump, and the horse is cantering disunited.*

the back becomes hollow and the hind legs are unable to engage when most needed.

JUMPING METHODS

I started jumping at the age of ten. This took place at boarding school, where I rode some rather hot ponies and found it a frightening experience. During the holidays I taught my own pony, which had not jumped previously, and despite the blind leading the blind it even led to some success at local shows.

How this was ever possible defies imagination, especially when I remember that it involved taking a backward seat over fences, holding on to a loop of string tied to the pommel of the saddle. My pony's tolerance was little short of miraculous, and its courage enormous. Some other juvenile competitors fared even worse, being tied on to their saddles by enthusiastic parents.

Just how outrageous this exploitation of ponies and children was did not reveal itself to me until later, when riding as a professional opened my eyes to the serious implications of these methods. At this time, the Italian forward seat was becoming better known, and was being taught in civilian riding schools. Anyone who has lived long enough to remember the early days of show-jumping will realise what a change it has made, not only in the rider's balance but in the freedom it gives to the horse's back, mouth and hindquarters.

After qualifying, I continued show-jumping in adult classes on a series of inexperienced mounts, some of which, in their excitement, bordered on the dangerous. At that time, the light rails and laths which were put on top of fences were the order of the day. These laths were easily displaced by the current of air created when the horse jumped, without their feet ever touching them. This led to the practice of rapping the horse's legs as a means of teaching it to pick them up as high as possible to avoid the half fault which each displaced lath accumulated. This practice does not make for happy jumping horses, only anxious ones which become tense and difficult when their tolerance is exploited in this way.

Another vogue at that time was the use of the standing martingale, further evidence of insufficient schooling. This held the nose down by means of the caveson noseband to which the martingale was attached at one end, being fixed to the girth at the other. When a horse has to have its head tied down in order to control it, something is sadly amiss. By fixing the horse's head irrevocably, the martingale limits the use of its body in taking off over the fence, and also on landing. The horse's head and neck are its means of balance and it needs this freedom to develop its jumping ability.

What happened in practice was that the horse set up resistance to the martingale. It could still pull up against this restraint, creating an unnatural build-up of muscle under its neck, a hollow back and tenseness throughout his body.

Recognition of this fact did not surface until riders began having trouble at the water jump, which was usually the last fence on a course. This was always built in the centre of the show ring and was arrived at by dashing pell mell towards it in order to gain enough power to clear the wide expanse of water.

It became obvious that this was impossible to do successfully if the horse's head was strapped down, so an ingenious

Fig 119   Jumping water needs full extension from the horse.

device appeared on the market which was attached to the standing martingale like a clip on a dog lead. When this was released it extended the martingale to allow the horse more freedom of its head and neck for the long jump. Executed from the saddle on a steamed-up horse raring to go, this operation was no mean feat, yet it was regularly seen as a preliminary to the climax at the end of the jumping round. The audience watched with bated breath as the horse circled about, the rider half-way out of the saddle trying to undo the gadget. Top-class show-jumping has seen many changes since then. Like other sports it has become highly specialised, and the scientific and logical techniques which build up a horse's athleticism are now recognised as being the most successful way of bringing out the best performance.

Before leaving these reflections on jumping methods, it is worth recalling the jumping lanes used by the army, where recruits were required to take off or put on their tunics while negotiating the jumps. This helped to develop their balance, ensuring that their hands were totally independent of the reins and not being used for security. These games were sometimes used in riding schools when jumping without saddles and reins. In some ways it is sad that the hazards involved in these techniques have stopped us using them.

THE APPROACH

Seamus Hayes, the former Irish show-jumper of international repute, is quoted by Lucy Rees in *The Horse's Mind* as saying:

The horse detests tension, for he must feel free and confident in his movement. The control of tension is the dominating factor in any sport.

This relaxation is what the following routines which lead to jumping are all about. They are the bricks which go to build a safe and sound platform from which further possibilities come within range. Everything that has been learnt so far is of value in this transitional stage. All experienced trainers recognise that flat work is a useful preparation for jumping and, in turn, these change of balance exercises can improve the horse's flat work and raise the standard of its dressage performance. The exercises consist of poles on the ground, over which the horse first learns to walk and then to trot. Initially, these poles are placed quite haphazardly in the schooling area, so the horse becomes accustomed to stepping over them with confidence.

When the horse starts stepping over the poles, it has to look where it is going. Consequently, it lifts its feet higher as it picks its way over them. The result is that it lowers its head to look at what it is doing, which helps it to make its back round and to bring its hind legs further underneath. This simple exercise actually puts the horse in the balance it requires to be able to jump. With this work its mind and body are progressively prepared for the practicality of leaving the ground. Jumping comes as the logical conclusion to a series of small obstacles, rather than as a sudden reaction to a hazard which appears in its path for no apparent reason.

The rider's balance must adapt to the more elevated steps of the horse, so the horse can swing its back and change its centre of gravity as well as feel free to use its head and neck. When actually jumping, the horse changes its centre of gravity quite dramatically as it takes off, becomes airborne, lands on the other side and rebalances itself for the next obstacle. When the rider is positioned to accommodate these variations, he or she will be able to go with the horse's movement without interfering with it.

The rider is responsible for the preparation of the horse's balance and direction in the approach to a jump, while the horse is responsible for the act of jumping itself and deciding where it needs to take off. When fences are approached with quiet confidence, there is every chance of the horse clearing them and thus gaining the extra confidence to enjoy jumping. When the horse is in balance, control is easier to maintain, which enables the rider to use all the ground between the fences in the best way and to keep the horse's attention on the jump. Approaches, turns and speed will also be best organised to suit the type of fence that has to be jumped. Time spent in improving the horse's performance in this way is well worthwhile when it is put to the test.

The approach to a jump has three phases. The first is one of preparation, where the pace at which the jumping is done is consolidated as thoroughly as it would be for a dressage test. It may be the canter or, for the young horse, the trot.

The second phase starts before the horse makes the turn into the approach. This is when we see riders cantering or

Fig 120   This horse is confident and active.

trotting their horses in circles before they start a round in order to settle them down and restore their balance. The turn to a fence is a critical part of the approach, since if it is unbalanced it will affect the horse's agility. If, on the other hand the turn is made with control, the horse is presented with the obstacle as advantageously as possible. This phase can be called the attentive riding stage, in which the horse is kept active and alert without losing its rhythm.

The last phase is the three strides in front of the fence which bring the horse to the take-off stage. It is during these last few strides that the rider may need to ride the horse assertively yet without disturbing its tempo. It is the horse's responsibility to decide where it needs to take off, not the rider's, and it is here that the rider must be right with the horse. The horse must be free to make the decision without feeling it is going to be disturbed by any

unexpected movement on the part of the rider. It must be remembered that the horse's view of the fence is very different to that of the rider's and, as the horse has to get its own body over the fence, plus the rider's weight, it is much better to let it make its own arrangements. Thus the horse learns to become a safe and reliable performer. Jumping in this way is called 'non-interventional', which implies that the rider is letting the horse choose its own take-off stride.

When a more experienced rider takes over this responsibility, it is known as using 'intervention'. The disadvantage of this method is that the horse becomes reliant on the rider and, if there is an error, it may not be able to get itself out of trouble in the same way as its more self-reliant counterpart. There is no doubt, however, that where there is a mutual understanding about the correct place for the take-off, the rider can intuitively help the horse to lengthen or shorten its stride in order to reach it. This is not so much active intervention as a sign that the rider's eye is developing discernment in judging pace and distance. Riders tend to become very concerned about their stride when jumping, but if attention is kept on the horse's rhythmical forward movements, the horse will be able to make the right decisions.

There are three phases in the approach to a jump and four phases when it comes to the jump itself. These are more clear-cut, being the take-off, the period of suspension, the landing and the next few strides. Looking at the jumping pattern in this way helps us to see the interrelationship of approach and actual jumping, followed by the recovery and repetition each time the horse faces a new obstacle. This helps to make a cohesive pattern of all the separate parts which each fence represents. If a course is ridden with this pattern in mind, it will have the purpose and flow so important to a successful and enjoyable performance.

The exercises which involve the use of poles can be looked upon as connecting the flat work of the dressage training to the techniques of jumping. It helps to think of them as a valuable activity in that movement can be in either direction. Once the horse has become used to single poles scattered anywhere in the schooling area, the degree of difficulty can gradually be increased until the horse is able to negotiate a row of parallel poles, beginning with three and increasing to six or more. These are placed about 1.3 metres (four feet) apart, depending on the horse's ability to meet them in such a way that it is able to step over them in the middle of its stride. The use of two poles only is not advisable because the horse

tends to jump them; this is not what is wanted at this stage.

When the horse begins this work, it should be allowed to walk quietly and slowly over the poles, picking its way and lowering its head to look at what it is doing. The steps will not be even and the horse may tap the poles, but if the rider leaves it alone it will soon learn to do it neatly and confidently. The object is to keep the horse calm and attentive. This gives it time to think what it is doing. The rider should sit lightly in the saddle to give the horse's back more freedom, and to permit it to lower its head and neck.

The horse finds it easier to trot over the poles, because the way that they are spaced suits its stride better and encourages it to swing over them easily. The rider will feel a distinct difference in the movement and should use rising trot to accommodate it.

The rider's awareness can be brought to bear on the way the horse uses its diagonal steps as it trots over the poles. To check whether there is any difference between them, ride with your eyes shut if you are brave enough and, as you make a practice run, ride on one diagonal and then change to the other the next time you come down over the poles. Some riders have found they can sense the footfall in their hands if they hold the foam balls.

When the horse is working actively with the poles, the swing in its back will be more pronounced, as one of my pupils found out. Jill had been working a novice horse which had very little spring in its stride over the trotting poles. After a few practice attempts, she came to the coach and said: 'My goodness, this is affecting my back. I can feel a pronounced diagonal swing'. When she was observed

Fig 121   This horse is rushing and its steps are flat.

Fig 122   The horse is calmer but the rider is behind the movement.

Fig 123   The rider is in balance – the horse is starting to lower its head and its steps are more elevated.

from behind, this was seen to be true, for the horse's movement was indeed affecting her own stiffness, providing what amounted to a remedial exercise for her back. The result of this was a marked improvement in the paces of this particular horse, which showed a bounciness it had not previously demonstrated.

Accuracy is just as important in jumping as it is in a dressage test, particularly in the turns that have to be made into fences and in changes of direction. When the horse is using the poles it should be directed straight down the centre of them. This is good practice for coming in to jumps at a later stage.

Another reason for working over poles in trot is that it is the pace which helps to develop the spring which is needed for take-off and to encourage the horse to use its back. Unlike the canter, where speed can become a factor, the trot enables the horse to bounce off its hind legs, since it

is easier to bring them together at the right moment. It is also easier for the horse to judge its take-off stride, which can reassure the rider, who often feels uncertain as the horse begins its jump.

When they start jumping, pupils can easily be over-instructed about the way they should sit in the saddle, and end up over-correcting or becoming confused. In some ways the less that is said the better, for some pupils do manage to get in tune with their horses when they jump, without being bombarded by too much advice.

Bill was a novice rider who was working his young horse over a line of poles. The coach then placed a small fence of crossed poles 2.7 metres (nine feet) beyond the last pole. The next time Bill came in he trotted his horse calmly down the poles and over the jump without any effort or loss of balance. He repeated this routine a few more times, then returned

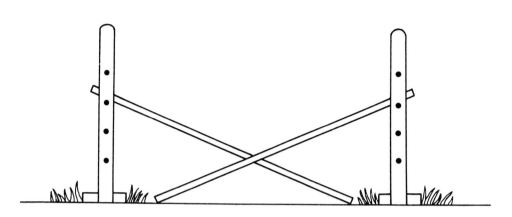

Fig 124   Crossed poles – an inviting fence for a horse.

to the coach to announce that he had never jumped before. The coach, who suspected this, said: 'All the better, because you have no preconceived ideas and can go with your horse naturally.' A horse which has had a good basic training will nearly always be able to jump a small fence like this when you ask it to.

When Bill went on to jump higher obstacles he needed to make some adjustments to his position in the saddle, which enabled him to go with his horse's movement when its trajectory over the jump increased.

Sometimes there is controversy about the correctness of the jumping seat, in terms of how long the stirrups should be and where to place the upper body to be in balance. Horses seem to have more confidence in a rider who intuitively moves with them rather than one who consciously puts himself or herself in place. A horse dislikes and is disturbed by a rider who is left behind in the movement over the fence, but dislikes

it even more when they are in front of it, so it is essential for the rider to keep the centre of gravity over that of the horse.

When the stirrups are shortened by one to three holes, depending on the size of jump and the shape of both horse and rider, a firmer base will be provided, so that the upper body can come forward and still be stable. This enables riders to make the seat lighter in the saddle as they put more weight on the stirrup irons and their legs. In this position, the hands are able to follow the movement of the horse's head and neck as it stretches, which means that a consistent yet flexible contact with the reins can be maintained.

In early training it is important not to raise the height of jumps too quickly, as widening a jump will naturally increase the height that the horse needs to use in order to clear it. This logical sequence can be developed by placing a second fence 5.4 metres (six yards) beyond the crossed poles. This allows for one non-jumping stride of canter which the

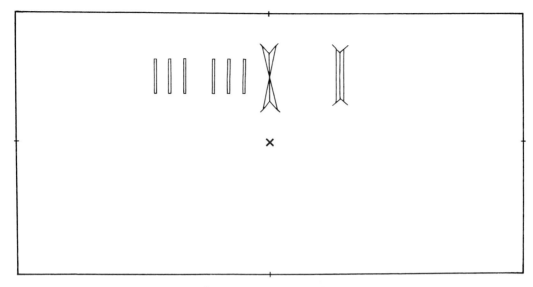

Fig 125   The use of six poles develops more activity in the
horse and is a variation which keeps its interest. They lead to a
small spread fence after one stride of canter.

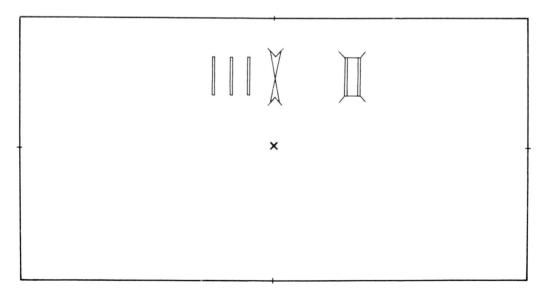

Fig 126   This layout introduces the horse to one non-jumping
stride of canter before the second fence.

horse will do naturally on landing after the first fence. At a later stage still, a third fence can be placed two non-jumping strides beyond the second one, thus teaching the horse to jump not only from trot but also from canter without any loss of calmness or control. When this training is consolidated it should be possible to canter a course of jumps in a quiet and competent manner.

Establishing the balance of both partners is the secret of enjoyable and successful jumping. Any loss of balance on the rider's part means either that they get left behind and interfere with the horse's back, mouth or hind legs, or get in front of the movement and fall on the shoulders of the horse, interfering with its take-off.

The horse finds this sudden shift of the rider's weight as it is about to come off the ground very disturbing indeed, and may result in its refusal to jump at all. This can be caused by the rider's anxiety to be with the horse at the right moment. Once the horse starts to pull up while coming into a fence, this tendency increases, putting the rider too far forward unless their balance is very stable. An extreme example of this, of course, is when the horse stops suddenly and the rider carries on over the horse's head.

REFUSALS

At some time or another, refusals are an inevitable part of the jumping experience,

Fig 127   This rider is behind the movement of the horse which causes it to hollow its back.

Fig 128   This rider is in balance and the horse has freedom to use its body.

Fig 129   The rider is in front of the movement.

and it is important to try to understand their causes. The horse is trying to tell us something when it does this. It may be that it has been faced with jumps that are too big, or that it has been jumped too much and become sour, or that it is frightened of the rider's interference at the wrong moment. There may have been an accident in the past which has left the horse with unpleasant associations. On the other hand, a wise and experienced horse may sometimes stop because it has arrived in front of a jump in such a way that it decides that it is safer not to jump. It is important to know when the horse is being sensible and to avoid giving a reprimand instead of a reward.

The horse's vision is another important factor when it comes to jumping. Though horses are thought to be colourblind, research suggests that they may find some colours more difficult to jump than others. Certainly, horses can have problems jumping from light into darkness, such as a fence leading from a sunny field into a dark wood.

Considering the way in which riders often deal with refusals, it is hardly surprising that the horse becomes more defensive. All too common is the situation where the rider whips the horse round once it has stopped, dashing back as fast as possible to take another long and speedy approach into the fence. This procedure is illogical for two reasons. In the first place, the horse wants to be taken away from the fence, not to try it again. Secondly, a long approach at speed provides the horse with every chance to plan another evasive strategy. If the approach is shortened and ridden in a more controlled manner, there is more chance of the horse arriving straight in front of the fence and being able to jump it.

Let us look at an alternative way of dealing with this problem. When the horse stops in front of a fence, do not expect it to jump from a standstill, since it cannot see it properly. Do not, however, take the horse away from the fence. Just let it stand for a few minutes until you are ready to teach it some obedience and awareness exercises. The aim is to recapture the horse's willingness to go forward.

You cannot employ these tactics if you are in a competition, but they are very effective whenever the chance is available to put them into practice. Your first aim is to get the horse to stand in front of the jump exactly in the centre, with its body at right angles to it. A horse who has refused will often be unwilling to do this, and will show resistance either by reining back or by swinging its quarters. It is important to deal quietly and firmly with whichever evasion the horse shows first. If the horse reins back, ask it to go forward one step, then pat it. If, on the other hand, it swings its quarters to one side, push them back with your opposite leg and pat the horse once again. Keep asking and rewarding in the same way as you have already established in your communication with your horse. When the horse realises that it is not being asked to jump or do anything else which is difficult, it will calm down and listen. When this happens you will be able to ask it to stand straight and calmly at the centre of the jump. You have achieved your first goal.

The next requirement is forward intention from the horse, so while it remains calm, use your legs very gently and notice its reaction. There must be no question of jumping from this position. What you may discover is that the horse

Fig 130 The horse is standing obediently and calmly in front of the fence.

will do one of three things. It may stretch its neck forward and down, or bunch its muscles in readiness, or pick up one or other foreleg. All these are positive indications on the horse's part, and whichever one it produces first needs immediate acknowledgement, for you only need one reaction from it.

This is the time to turn quietly away from the fence to prepare a new approach in a controlled way. The chances are that the horse will now jump it willingly, for there has been no association of refusal and punishment, only a quiet and precise explanation which the horse has had time to understand.

A few years ago I was taking a jumping rally when a problem arose with a particular horse and rider at a combination fence. The horse, which had been jumping well, refused on coming into the first obstacle. The routine I have just explained was implemented. It took some time because the horse was upset. The moment came when it stood calmly at the centre of the fence and indicated its willingness to go forward. The rider then made a new approach and jumped the

Fig 131   This horse has made a gesture of forward intention.

two fences without any hesitation. Before the rally the rider's father had laid bets on the horse not jumping, as it had previously fallen at a double when competing at a show and, until that day, no one had been able to induce it to jump another combination fence.

OTHER PROBLEMS

No one can ride or jump faultlessly all the time, and no one is more long-suffering than the horse. It can tolerate an occasional lapse but not a succession of lapses to which its answer will be to stop jumping. Resolving this dilemma means retracing your steps to discover where confidence began to falter.

Any tension that arises during jumping will show in the rein line. This should ideally be a gentle curve from your shoulder, through your elbow and hand, to the horse's mouth. If this line is broken when jumping, the rider's weight will probably be supported on the horse's neck, and the rider could well be too far forward as a result. To counteract this, you can practise putting your reins in one hand a few strides before take-off and holding the free hand forward as if you are offering a gift. This movement helps to keep the hands independent and allows the flow of movement from the horse to go through the rider. Holding balls in your hands is again useful, as they register tenseness in the hands at the critical moment and help you to pay attention to this, allowing the body to adapt naturally.

Trusting your own body may seem more difficult than trusting that of the horse, but when you do, resistance is

Fig 132   This rider is going with the movement of the horse.

dissipated and your performance can reach levels beyond your expectations. Confidence is usually built up during these basic exercises, but there are exceptions when pupils have admitted to feeling anxious about doing pole work. Some dislike the poles in front of the fence, finding them distracting; so do certain horses. Others dislike going over poles wherever they are placed, which proves the danger of being dogmatic about anything. Pupils who are allowed to choose the siting of fences and poles, either in relation to one another or on their own, provide interesting designs, distances and results. If calmness and confidence are the outcome and safety is not endangered, then all is well and it can only be a constructive experiment.

The rider's attention should also be on the preparation and presentation of the horse for the fence beyond the one that is currently being approached. This will include the turns on which successful jumping so often depends. Riders often start looking for the angle too late and, as a result, turn too wide and unbalance the horse in trying to correct their approach. The poor horse arrives unprepared, and has to extricate itself as best it can.

It is important to pay attention to the process involved in reaching the correct take-off zone with your horse in a balanced state, so that it has every opportunity to choose the best position. The rider has enough to do in directing the horse's energy and choosing the best possible line to the fence without worrying about anything else. The end result will then look after itself, because the horse has been helped and not hindered by the rider.

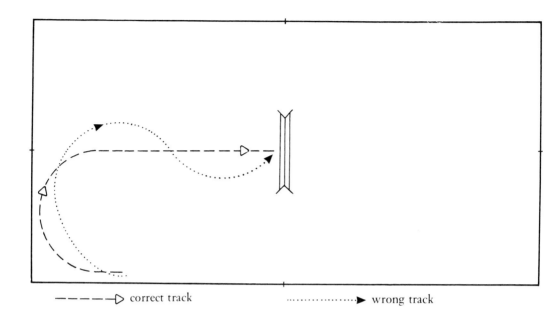

————▷ correct track   ·················▶ wrong track

Fig 133 Correct and incorrect lines of approach.

Fear and anxiety can often mar what might otherwise be promising progress in learning to jump. One of the signs of tenseness is the clenched fist, and if the fists are tight the tension can usually also be located internally, perhaps in the chest or the abdomen. The horse, being the recipient of much of this tension, knows all about either sort of symptom. The clenched fist syndrome is the result of a perceived threat or insecurity, clinging on or keeping something to yourself, a sign of grim determination. Identifying the background to this tightness, which indirectly affects the horse's mouth, will help to take the strain off the rein.

This analogy may give you food for thought in other areas and, to counteract this symptom of tenseness, you could consider the implications of the physical feeling which clenching your fists gives you as well as the mental counterpart.

What words or thoughts come to mind as you consciously do this? You can then review the opposite situation when you deliberately open your hands and once again review your thoughts as you do so. You could find this a liberating and revealing experience. After all, it is not only the reins we tend to hold in this way when we are under pressure but also the steering-wheel of the car.

In her book *Riding with your Mind*, Mary Wanless suggests making a friend of fear and giving it an identity, so that it can be parked on one side as a spectator. This concept might well appeal to some people and help them feel that they can transform it into something more positive.

One of the most relevant and descriptive comments made by pupils is that of feeling at a very high pitch. This musical reference is very apt, because when the voice is used in this state it will tend to induce tension in the throat and mouth.

This introduces another awareness game, which some people prefer to do using numbers. Ask yourself what note of the scale relates to the way you feel. You might like to relate the note to a particular colour. By associating red with high doh, for example, the rest of the colour spectrum can be related accordingly. Visualising colours can alter your breathing from the excited hurried respiration that red can induce to the tranquillity of indigo or violet.

Fear is always lurking under the surface, and we are usually most afraid of the unknown and of frightening experiences from the past. On my first skiing lesson at the age of sixty-five, I fell and broke my leg. Taking up skiing again after that seemed very unlikely, but then an Inner Game coaching course I went on included dry skiing in the syllabus.

I explained my apprehension to the coach, who suggested I went along and took things as they came. I was not pressurised in any way, but questioned as to my feelings about and reasons for the fear. When I arrived at the lesson I was feeling sick about the prospect of skiing again, thinking things like 'I must make myself', and, 'Don't be such a coward, you're wasting an opportunity.'

Finally, I decided to put on my skis and walk about, but found that this did not lessen my apprehension. At the bottom of the slope I was overcome by a terrifying feeling of instability and loss of control. I don't think I have ever felt so paralysed. My main thoughts were that a repetition of the injury would occur, with all its inconveniences and loss of independence. Then there was what people would say about a silly old

woman who could not learn from experience.

None of the ski instructors was able to help, but finally a friend, who had just ski'd successfully for the first time that afternoon, came to practise her coaching on me. We went through all the Inner Game rigmarole once more, and then she said: 'How would you turn if you were on a horse?' Immediately my mind switched to the problem. 'How would I?' I asked myself. The answer was that I needed to turn my skis just as I would turn a horse by moving it round its haunches in a pivot. This I did successfully, and the spell was broken. I found myself happily skiing down a small slope in no time at all. This experience also proved that you do not always need an expert to help you.

Here is a personal visualisation which many people find effective. Identify your fear or each aspect of it by colour, shape or even personification, and put them all into an imaginary half-filled balloon. As you breathe out, blow the balloon up until you feel it is full of air and can be sealed up and allowed to rise into space until it disappears.

The Gallop

To round off the natural riding options now opening up to the rider, the gallop must be mentioned. Too often a horse is galloped in an uncontrolled and haphazard manner with little regard for safety or for the soundness of the horse. As the horse increases its speed, balance must still be maintained. The gallop is a pace of four time, and comes about by the second diagonal beat of the canter being divided. The result of this is that the

Fig 134   The gallop sequence: off hind on ground.

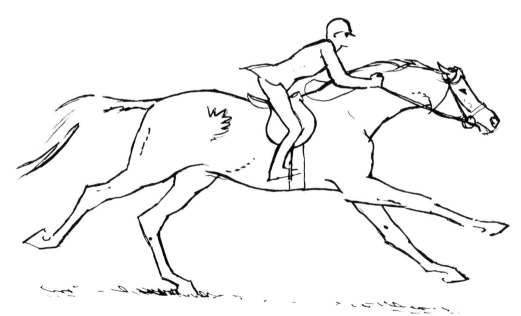

Fig 135   Near hind.

Fig 136   Off fore.

Fig 137   Near fore.

Fig 138   In the air.

horse will move its legs in the following sequence if it is leading on the off fore: near hind, off hind, near fore, off fore; after this there is a period of suspension, just as there is in canter.

When the horse is galloping, its centre of gravity moves further forward as it extends its stride. The rider will need to be more forward to align with the horse's centre of gravity and, when racing, to reduce wind resistance. When we talk about a horse getting into its stride, this indicates the significance of rhythm, especially when staying power is important.

Racehorses are not all ambidextrous in relation to their leading legs, which means that trainers often have to choose race tracks to suit their horses, rather than assuming that a horse will be able to run well whether it is a left- or right-handed circuit.

I have a pupil who trains her own racehorses. On this occasion she brought a particular horse for the basic schooling described in this book. The horse was very stiff, restricted in its paces, and difficult to turn in one particular direction, which meant it could only lead on its near fore leg in canter. In a few lessons there was a marked improvement, and with the patient practice which went on at home the horse became a delightful ride and a consistently successful racehorse.

When it comes to galloping your horse, make sure that it is fit enough to gallop. Then you can enjoy the benefit of controlling the power and speed of this exhilarating pace.

By now the warp and weft of working out a partnership with your horse will have become a fascinating journey of discovery, weaving a pattern of recurring themes with endless permutations, not unlike a tapestry or a musical composition. Riding is a real art form, though too few riders are willing to utilise their horse's full potential.

If you are content with a push-button horse that walks, trots, canters and turns rather stiffly, you are missing much of the pleasure of riding. The difference between a horse which moves like a clockwork mouse and one which dances along with a pliant body is like the difference between a wooden bed and a spring mattress.

This difference is largely dependent on the rider's awareness, which is what this book has been about. It is not just about physical development; it is just as much to do with our mental attitude, which has such a profound influence on the horse. When our senses are blunted by the stimuli of modern living, we need even stronger ones to make us pay attention. We can so easily lose the innate awareness of a child who notices fascinating and significant detail. The sum of these details is always greater than the whole.

Natural riding includes natural jumping which, although it is not a natural attribute of the horse, can with training appear as if it were an innate talent. When this happens, the horse will leave us in no doubt of its enjoyment. As the Greek, Xenophon, said in 400 BC, as quoted in Gunnar Hedlund's *This is Riding:*

When a rider has managed to make his horse look as if it were free and showing off, then he is riding a horse who looks happy, proud and beautiful.

The horse is the epitome of many special qualities which we are privileged to experience through its generosity and friendship. The horse accepts us as we are, so that we always know where we stand. The horse tolerates our deficiencies and teaches us the truth, and through discovering the horse we see ourselves more clearly. In this way the horse becomes a miraculous medium through which we recognise reality with all its enriching possibilities.

Appendix

The following forms are used to provide feedback from pupils and coaches and help them to clarify their thoughts in a way that makes information gained easier to retain. Anyone who has difficulty expressing themselves will find they can do so in this simple way and are often surprised how it unlocks ideas which can then be added to the completed form.

Instructors

Please tick where applicable and add anything extra about any question on another sheet of paper.

What do you enjoy about teaching?
helping others – pupil   .....
the horse   .....
learning from pupil/horse   .....
anything else   .....

What do you find most difficult?
large group   .....
small children   .....
jumping lesson   .....
being heard   .....
controlling class   .....
seeing faults   .....
correcting them   .....
authority, control   .....
anything else   .....

What have you achieved this weekend?
understanding of pupil   .....
understanding of horse   .....
understanding of yourself   .....

learning difficulties   .....
organising a ride   .....
being understood   .....
creating improvement – pupil   .....
creating improvement – horse   .....

Which are the three most important?
relaxation   .....
one thing at a time   .....
not trying   .....
trying too hard   .....
being calm   .....
involving pupil   .....
having time   .....
confidence   .....
authority   .....

Write down any further ideas and reactions you may have.

Pupils

What do you find difficult in lessons? Tick three.
not hearing   .....
not understanding   .....
not having time to fix exercise in your mind   .....
doing too much at once   .....
paying attention   .....
too much to remember   .....
feeling stupid   .....
being shouted at   .....
getting tired   .....
being worried about your horse .....
not doing well   .....

Which three do you enjoy most?
   dressage   .....
   jumping   .....
   cross country   .....
   schooling in general   .....
   being taught   .....
   going for rides   .....
   looking after your horse   .....

What do you like most about your horse?
How do you relate to the coach?
Please add anything else you want, about anything.

Awareness Questions

Effective coaching questions are those that provoke description rather than judgement, analysis or speculation, i.e. those that result in increased awareness rather than additional clutter.

- What's happening now?
- How would you like it to be ideally?
- What needs to change to get there?
- What's preventing that?
- How will you know if you are successful?
- When does it happen?
- What have you tried?
- Does that always happen?
- What happens?
- What have you done in the past?
- How committed are you to that?
- What do you want to do?
- When will you do it?
- What have you seen so far?
- How would you rate it 0–10?
- What would make it a 10?
- Is that possible?
- Is that realistic?
- Who is involved?
- Are you going to do it?
- What's the first step?
- If you could do anything, what would you do?
- Is there anything that could stop that happening?
- What could get in the way?
- What obstacles do you foresee?
- How can I help/support you?

Bibliography

Clarke, Bransby *Think Yourself Slim* Foulsham & Co. Ltd. (1988)

Edwards, Betty *Drawing on the Right Side of the Brain* Wm. Collins & Co. Ltd. (1979)

Gallwey, Timothy W. *Inner Tennis* Random House Inc. (1976)

Gallwey, Timothy W. *The Inner Game of Golf* Jonathan Cape (1981)

Gallwey, Timothy W. and Kriegel, Bob *Inner Ski-ing* Bantam Books (1977)

Gelb, Michael *Body Learning* Aurum Press (1981)

Green, Barry with Gallwey, Timothy W. *The Inner Game of Music* Pan Books (1986)

Hedlund, Gunnar *This is Riding* George G. Harrap & Co. Ltd. (1981)

Maltz, Maxwell M.D. *Psycho Cybernetics* Thorsons Publishers Ltd. (1986)

Marshall, Lyn *Instant Stress Cure* Century (1988)

Rees, Lucy *The Horse's Mind* Stanley Paul (1984)

Richards, Lockie *Dressage* David & Charles (1975)

Roon, Karin *The New Way to Relax* Cedar Books (1951)

Shone, Ronald *Creative Visualisation* Thorsons Publishers Ltd. (1984)

Smythe, R.H. *The Mind of the Horse* Country Life Ltd. (1965)

Stevens, Chris *Alexander Technique* Optima (1987)

Swift, Sally *Centred Riding* William Heinemann Ltd. (1985)

Syer, John and Connelly, Christopher *Sporting Body Sporting Mind* Cambridge University Press (1984)

Wanless, Mary *Ride with your Mind* Methuen London Ltd. (1987)

Willcox, Sheila *The Event Horse* Pelham Books (1973)

Index